Running Successful

Projects

in the

Voluntary Sector

A guide for project people
in the
charitable and voluntary sectors

Stuart Kelly

Published by:

3rd Sector Skills
43 Croydon Road
Penge
London
SE20 7TJ

Email books@3rdsectorskills.com
www.3rdsectorskills.com

First published 2012

ISBN 978-0-9571473-0-0

3rd Sector Skills

Table of Contents

Preface **1**

    WARNINGS 1
    ANOTHER WARNING 1
    PICTURES AND DIAGRAMS 2

Introduction **3**

    DEFINITION OF A PROJECT 3
    DIMENSIONS OF A PROJECT 4
    THE GOLDEN RULES 6
    TOOLS TO HELP YOU 7
    PAPERWORK 8
    PROJECT MANAGEMENT MODELS 9
    USING THIS BOOK 10
    SIX STAGE MODEL 11

STAGE: DEFINE - Defining your project **12**

    A PROJECT IS BORN 12
    PROJECT OBJECTIVES 13

People in projects **17**

    STAKEHOLDERS 17
    PROJECT TEAM 18

Considering the options **20**

    FEASIBILITY 20
    OPPORTUNITIES AND THREATS 20
    COSTS AND BENEFITS 21
    PUTTING THE COST/BENEFIT ANALYSIS TOGETHER 21
    DISCOUNTED CASH FLOW 22

Risks **23**

    RISK AND CONTINGENCY PLANNING 23
    PROJECT RISKS 23
    IMPACT ANALYSIS 24
    RISK REGISTER 26
    STRATEGIES FOR DEALING WITH RISK 26
    THE BIGGEST RISK OF ALL - CHANGE 27

Bringing it all together **29**

    PROJECT BRIEF 29
    CONTENTS OF A TYPICAL PROJECT BRIEF 29
    THE PROJECT BRIEF AS A FUND-RAISER 30
    PROJECT KICK-OFF 30
    THE "TO HECK WITH IT" MOMENT 31

STAGE: PLAN - Planning your project **32**

    WHERE DO I START? 32
    PRODUCTS/DELIVERABLES 32
    IDENTIFY KEY STEPS 34

Scheduling   **36**

    STARTING OFF – THE SALAMI TECHNIQUE   36
    HOW TO REPRESENT THE PROJECT   37
    LINKING TASKS   39
    OVERLAPPING TASKS   40
    PUTTING THE SCHEDULE TOGETHER   41

How long will it take?   **42**

    START AND FINISH TIMES   42
    CRITICAL PATH   43
    FINDING THE CRITICAL PATH   44

Resources   **52**

    ADDING RESOURCES TO A SCHEDULE   52
    LEVELLING   52
    AN EXAMPLE OF LEVELLING   54
    SCHEDULE CHECKLIST   58

Budget planning   **60**

    FULL COST RECOVERY   60
    PLAN FOR QUALITY   60
    PUTTING THE BUDGET TOGETHER   61
    CONTINGENCY   63
    YOUR FIRST DRAFT   64
    SOFTWARE – A VERY BRIEF MENTION   64

STAGE: TEAM BUILDING - Project teams   **66**

    A GOOD PROJECT MANAGER   66
    YET MORE THINGS TO BE GOOD AT   67
    PROJECT TEAM   68
    DEALING WITH SENIOR MANAGEMENT   69
    BELBIN'S TEAM ROLES   70

STAGE: CONTROL - Controlling your project   **71**

    MONITORING AS CONTROL   71
    LOG BOOK   71
    WHAT DO YOU MONITOR AGAINST?   71
    QUESTIONS TO ASK   72
    MANAGEMENT BY WALKING AROUND (MBWA)   73
    WHAT TO LOOK FOR   73
    PAPERWORK   74

Tracking progress   **75**

    PROJECT STATUS REPORTS   75
    SOFT REPORT   75
    TRACKING PROGRESS   76
    IS THE BUSINESS CASE STILL VALID?   77

Project meetings   **78**

    SUCCESSFUL MEETINGS   78
    PROJECT REVIEW MEETING AGENDA   80
    ALTERNATIVE WAYS OF HOLDING MEETINGS   81

Maintaining the balance   **83**

CHANGES 83
CHANGE CONTROL 83
THE CHANGE CONTROL MANTRA 84

STAGE: COMMUNICATIONS - Project communications 85

MANAGING COMMUNICATIONS DURING THE PROJECT 85
TYPES OF COMMUNICATION 85
WEB BASED SYSTEMS 86
COMMUNICATION PLAN 87
EFFECTIVE COMMUNICATION 87

STAGE: REVIEW - Reviewing your project 88

REVIEWING THE PLAN 88
REVIEWING THE RISK LOG AND IDENTIFYING PROBLEMS 88
REVIEWING THE BUDGET 88
REVIEWING THE NEED FOR THE PROJECT 90
PROBLEMS 91

Dealing with problems 92

PROBLEM SOLVING IN SEVEN EASY STEPS 92
CHANGES 93

STAGE: HANDOVER & EXIT 95

WHAT IS HANDED OVER AND WHEN? 95
PLAN FOR A SUCCESSFUL CONCLUSION 95
DEALING WITH UNRESOLVED ISSUES 95
ACCEPTANCE CERTIFICATE 96
CLOSURE 96

Evaluating the project 98

QUESTIONS TO ASK 98
DON'T FILE AND FORGET 98
WRITE IT UP – THE PORTFOLIO OF SUCCESS 98
DISMANTLING THE TEAM 99
SELF DEVELOPMENT FROM A PROJECT 99

Project management software 100

SOFTWARE PRODUCTS 100
SOFTWARE IS EXPENSIVE? 101
SOFTWARE SAVES TIME? 101
SOFTWARE'S TRUMP CARD 101
DON'T PLAN AT THE COMPUTER 102
SOFTWARE FEATURES 102

Data security 103

HOW TO BACKUP 103
RESTORING DATA 104

Working with large projects 105

IMPACT ON THE PROJECT MANAGER 105
NEW THINGS TO CONSIDER WHEN YOU HAVE A LARGE PROJECT 105
RISK AND CONTINGENCY PLANNING 106
PROJECT TEAM 106

Communications	106
Planning	107
Keeping track of problems	107
Project issues	107
Change control	109
Managing multi-site projects	109
Summary	110
Working with multiple projects	**111**
Keeping on top of multiple projects	111
Managing people	111
Juggling priorities	111
It's fun	112
What Can Go Wrong	**113**
Unsure of objectives/deliverables	113
Nearly met objectives	113
Ran late/exceeded budget	113
What next?	**115**
Appendix 1 – Exercises	**117**
Appendix 2 – Discounted Cash Flow	**123**
An example	123
Example 1 – simple method	123
Discounted Cash Flow made easy (!)	125
Example 2 - Discounted Cash Flow	127
Internal rate of return (IRR)	129
Compare two options	129
IRR and discount rates	131
NPV vs. project life	131
Summary	132
Appendix 3 – Additional resources	**133**
Appendix 4 - Table of Discount Factors	**136**
Appendix 5 – Answer to critical path exercise	**137**
Index to tables	**138**
Index to figures	**139**
INDEX	**141**

Preface

What is a project manager? Is it some strange creature poring over mystical charts who comes to berate you for being late delivering your task? Well, yes probably – we've all met people like this.

But being a little more serious, YOU are a project manager – yes, you!

Every time you put a series of tasks together with some sort of budgetary constraint and a timetable you're running a project. A celebratory meal like a birthday dinner is a classic project. There are certain ingredients that must be prepared in a given order to be ready to serve together at a set time. If you're preparing a Christmas dinner it's no good at all putting the Brussels sprouts on to cook at the same time as you put the turkey in the oven (unless of course, you like Brussels sprouts which have the consistency of soup).

In your working life managing a project is a more serious undertaking, and in order to do it successfully you really need a framework, some processes and procedures and some thought.

It's probably fair to say that most of us 'drift' in to project management. One day we suddenly wake up to the fact that we are managing projects and have been doing so for some time. We've struggled through, inventing processes on the fly, and we realise that "there must be an easier way to do this". That's when we log on to Amazon to look for a book or start leafing through the training brochures.

The purpose of this book is to provide you with a framework and introduce some useful processes, procedures, tips and tricks.

Warnings

1. We all have different personalities and work in different ways. What follows worked and works for me. Some of it will work for you too, and I encourage you to use it. Some of it may feel uncomfortable. If it does, don't use it. Look around for alternatives on the web or in other books. When you find something you like, use it.

2. You cannot learn to project manage from a book or from a training course. It's like saying you can learn to ride a bicycle from a book. What you can do is understand the processes involved, what to look out for, etc, and then apply them in your work – that's where the real learning takes place.

This book is intentionally light hearted. Project management can be fun (yes I know, you can see my anorak on the back of the door) and there are few things more satisfying than completing a project on time and on budget and thinking "I made that happen".

Another warning

The material in this book applies to projects of all sizes. Should you follow all these principles for all sizes of projects? Yes, you should, but you need to keep it in proportion. For example, you don't need a formal project brief, plan, risk register, etc for the Christmas dinner project but you should still think like a project manager when you're planning it. All the stuff in this book is scalable, and you should use it appropriately to the size and complexity of the project you're working on.

Pictures and Diagrams

A lot of the pictures and diagrams plus other useful templates mentioned in this book are available to download from the 3rd Sector Skills website[1], where there is also a blog for that strange creature – the third sector project manager.

Enjoy yourself!

---

[1] www.3rdsectorskills.com

Introduction

Projects are now a fact of life for organisations in the voluntary and community sector. Changing patterns of funding mean that it's becoming common for such organisations to develop their work and secure funding by developing specific projects.

This means that voluntary organisations have to be more professional about how they manage projects, for two reasons. Firstly, to make sure they deliver what they want to deliver to their clients; and secondly, to demonstrate to their funders that they are using the money in an effective way.

An organisation that manages projects effectively, and can demonstrate it, will do well and will find it easier to attract more projects, and should find it easier to comply with funders' monitoring requirements.

This book describes the concepts of project management with some thoughts on how they apply to the third sector. It is intended as a practical guide so it's not full of theory. It was developed from my successful course in project management.

What follows in this book applies to ALL projects no matter how big or small, and whatever their subject. But I urge you not to follow it all slavishly - some of the ideas and processes are more appropriate than others for different projects. For example, you don't need to be too formal about inter-team communication if you only have a couple of team members and you all work in the same office. But if your team is geographically spread you will need to take much more care over how you communicate with them, and they with you. Equally, you don't need a 40 page project brief to cope with a small project. The important idea here is to scale the processes sensibly.

Another point to make here is that a lot of voluntary organisations aren't big enough to have dedicated project managers. It is entirely possible, even very likely, that you are project manager, office manager, scheme administrator and lots more. If this is the case, please don't be irritated when I say things like '...when you hand the project over to the operational manager...' and you are both project and operational manager. Think of it as which hat are you wearing. I have always found this approach useful because it allows some clarity of thought.

Take what you need from this book and any other source material you read, and apply the information in a way that suits you and helps you to perform effectively.

Definition of a project

Before we go any further let's agree on what a project is or isn't. If I were delivering this material as a training course to you in person this is where I'd go to the flipchart and make you come up with ideas. But since I'm not, I offer here a good definition of a project.

> **A project is a one-off, non-repeated activity or set of tasks, which achieves clearly stated objectives within a time limit.**

From this definition you can see that a project is a set of non-routine activities with a beginning and an end. This project is inflicting a particular change on the world. When the project's finished, the world will not be the same. And because there is change, there is always some risk or uncertainty and, as we shall see, managing the risks is a major part of a project manager's workload.

There's an implication in the definition that a project has a supplier and a customer. If you're putting a new day centre together, then your clients can be considered as your customers. So, too, can your funders. If you're working for a large charity and putting in a new payroll system, then your customers could be your staff, your HR department, etc. Sometimes it's not easy to identify who is who, but it's really important to keep this concept in mind, as we shall see later when we consider the project's stakeholders.

The major difference between a project and any other sort of activity is the 'handing over of the keys'. I have this image in my mind of the project manager at the end of the project handing over a bunch of keys to her customer, turning her back and walking away – the project is complete. Not all projects have keys but the concept is worth holding on to. A project finishes and you walk away from it. Walking away from it in a sensible and controlled way is the subject of a later chapter. Again, if you are both project and operational manager, it's still worth thinking like this. It makes it easier to close down the project properly and move on.

Projects usually involve teams of people working together who don't normally work together, which can be fun, and there are invariably constraints put on the work, time and/or budget.

What is a project?

Imagine that CheapCo are building a new superstore in your town. Building the store is clearly a project. There is a definable change that CheapCo are inflicting on the world. The store isn't there now but it will be one day. There is a set of tasks to achieve the overall objective, there is clearly a budget and there is a timescale. At some time somebody will hand over a set of keys to someone else and that first someone will walk away from the building. The project will be complete.

Now what about running the store? Assuming it's not open 24 hours a day you could argue that each individual day is a project because each day is different to the one before. I think this is stretching the definition to breaking point because the day to day issues are so similar. Running the store is an operational issue and because the skills involved are different, I argue that it isn't a project.

Building the new CheapCo involves all sorts of people who would not normally come together: architects, planners, builders, etc. Once the store is open and running these people are no longer needed.

Dimensions of a project

Any project is a juggling act between time, budget and scope.

Time

This is pretty obvious. Every project will have a time element. This may be a 'brick wall' date that you just cannot miss, perhaps a well-publicised launch date where missing it would cause your organisation deep embarrassment; or the introduction of a new payroll system that has to be in and working by the end of the financial year. It might be a self-imposed target. If you've worked through the plan and you can complete your project by a certain date, missing this date would dent your pride but would not seriously inconvenience the organisation. The circumstances of your project determine how flexible you can be with time.

Budget

Budgets are tight – fact. In the voluntary sector there is never a surplus of money so compromising the budget is not to be taken lightly. It's rarely possible to extract more money from your customer. More often than not you just have to make do with what you have. However there are always ways to tinker with the budget. For example if you budgeted for a member of staff from month 1 but did not appoint until month 3 you have the unspent salary as a contingency. On the flip side, presumably you needed that person in month 1, so you have other issues with the work that didn't get done. But you may be able to use that contingency in a useful way.

Scope

The scope of a project is essentially what you're trying to deliver.

If our project is to deliver a writing instrument we may start off looking to deliver a Waterman fountain pen. In my opinion such a pen is a work of art, beautiful to look at and to hold and a joy to write with. But as time goes by and things start to go wrong, it's important to remember that our objective is to deliver a writing instrument and not a Waterman fountain pen. In order to deliver our project on time, we look at the scope and realise that we can still deliver a writing instrument if we select a Parker biro. It's still a quality product, writes well, is reliable and fit for purpose, albeit in a less elegant way. We have not compromised the quality of the product, but we have reduced the scope of the project.

We can apply this (admittedly strange) metaphor to our voluntary sector projects. If time and budget conspire against us then as long as we deliver the "writing instrument" we have delivered on the project. The worst thing to deliver would be half a fountain pen.

Consider a website project. Let's say the original concept was to have an all-singing, all-dancing site with lots of fancy features. If the project starts to run behind schedule you can recover the time by reducing the "scope" of the product. This doesn't mean you compromise with the information on the site but you could take out some of the fancy extras. This would reduce the amount of work and therefore could bring you back on schedule. It is this sort of scope compromise that is possible and acceptable and which works.

This sort of approach may also give you the opportunity to run a follow-up project; in this case you might "enhance" the website, to include features you've had to postpone as well as exciting new features!

--- ☆ ☆ ☆ ---

The job of project manager is to deliver the project on time, on budget and to the full scope. As the project develops real life will start to deviate from your plan and you will find you may need to compromise one of these three to recover your programme.

Figure 1 – Dimensions of a project

The golden rules

I have a couple of golden rules which have served me very well and I recommend them to you.

This is the first rule and if there could only be one rule, this would be it.

RULE 1 - NO SURPRISES

The very best project managers know what is going on. They find out by being with the people doing the work, talking to them, understanding what's happening and what the risks and issues are at first hand. Because they are on top of things they know what is happening in the project, what is coming up, what is likely to go wrong, and what they can do about it if it does.

Adopting this rule means you can sleep at night without worrying about what might be lurking in the future waiting for a good moment to ruin your day. Believe me, the last thing you want is for your chief executive/chair of trustees/whoever to call you and tell you of some disaster that's befallen your project. The ideal scenario is they call you to tell you and you reply that you are aware of the situation and have taken the appropriate actions to recover. How impressive is that?

You need to know what is going on all the time, be able to predict when something is about to go wrong, and have a plan ready to recover from it. You don't get that by sitting at your desk. Get out there!

RULE 2 - KISS

This is not an invitation to get amorous; it's an acronym for Keep It Simple, Stupid!

The goal of a project manager is to get the job done, not to generate tons of paper or hours of meetings. Paper and meetings are necessary but they're not the objective! The simpler you keep things the easier they are to keep track of and the fewer surprises you'll have. It's all too easy to get side-tracked into producing lots of reports and plans and stuff. Don't! Keep sight of the purpose of the project and remember what you are there to deliver.

Tools to help you

There are only 3 tools you need to be a successful project manager

1.   Structured approach
2.   Pencil
3.   Paper

You need a structured approach to make sure you cover everything you need to cover in the right order, and you need to write some stuff down. That's it. All the other tools that are available, including software, have the potential to make your life easier – sometimes. Software enables you to put all the information in one place and is a great help to schedule the project. But if your project is small, then using some of the more sophisticated tools can just make your life harder. We will cover software in more detail later (page 100); we're still in the introduction!

Stuart's software tips

Even if you're not going to use project management software to manage the project it can be a good idea to produce the project plan using it – the pictures and diagrams that it generates look really impressive, and if you're bidding for funding they make your organisation look really professional. If it helps you get the grant, go for it.

AND…. Never pay full price for your software. If you're a registered charity there are plenty of organisations out there that will sell you software at considerable discount. Check the 3rd Sector Skills website[2] for some links.

Methodology

A methodology is a set of processes that together give you a structured way of running a project. It's this structured approach that helps you bring order to managing a project.

Big industry has developed its own methodologies over the years and usually uses them to good effect. In the third sector, PRINCE2 is rapidly becoming a standard methodology. It is a process driven approach to project management. If you see your career staying with project management you may want to consider doing the PRINCE2 courses and getting the qualifications. The learning will certainly help you with your current job and the qualification will help your CV to get through the first sift when you're looking for something new.

This book describes a methodology which is pragmatic and which has shown itself to work for small to medium sized projects. It can easily be extended to cope with larger projects

---

[2] www.3rdsectorskills.com/resources/software

and we'll look at this towards the end of the book. Although some of the terms may be a little different, nothing here contradicts anything in PRINCE2.

Paperwork

Paperwork is essential to a successful project because projects are run by people, for people. And people are sneaky, have selective memories and hidden agendas; you don't want to be caught out.

You need some stuff written down. You can't remember everything. In fact there's a definite limit on what you can remember. I've always liked the story about Albert Einstein who (it is said) could not remember his own phone number. "I can always look it up in the directory" was his response when questioned. He didn't clutter his mind with stuff he didn't have to remember. I like that approach and so I write down stuff I need to know but don't need to remember. And the stuff I might need to know in a hurry I carry with me.

Customers will try to slip things past you and claim that they were in the specification all along; but if you have a good project spec, signed by the customer...

Project staff will claim they didn't know they were supposed to do this or that; but if you have a good definition of tasks...

You must keep formal records to help the project run smoothly, both for the organisation and to preserve your own sanity. But you should keep them only to a level appropriate to the scale of the project. They need to be sufficiently detailed to enable someone else to take over the project should you fall under a bus on the way home tonight. And they should be sufficiently detailed to enable you to satisfy your funders and to use to justify your expertise when it comes to bidding for the next project.

Remember, despite all the regulation that has come our way in the last few years, paperwork is your *servant*, not your master. It needs to be reminded about that from time to time.

You must have a

- project brief (or project specification – there are lots of names for this document)
- project plan
- risk log/register
- issue log/register
- stakeholder log/register (not mandatory, but a really good idea)
- log book

It can be useful to have other stuff as well but I believe these six are the minimum for the project. With them you know what you have to do (project brief), how you are going to do it (and with whom, and when and where – the project plan), what you need to look out for (risk register) and what the potential problems are (issue log). The stakeholder log reminds you who is involved and their agenda and the log book is a notebook that you keep and use it to note down conversations, telephone calls, notes at meetings, etc. It will be a sort of project diary and will help you keep on top of everything.

As the size and complexity of the project increases, it helps to have more written down because there's only so much any project manager can keep in mind all the time. The number of different documents you have and the size of each document depends on the size and complexity of the project. There is no right or wrong answer.

Project management models

There are quite a number of models which are used as the basis of project management tools and techniques.

The one that I favour, and on which this book is based, is the six stage model. There's a diagram of the model on page 11.

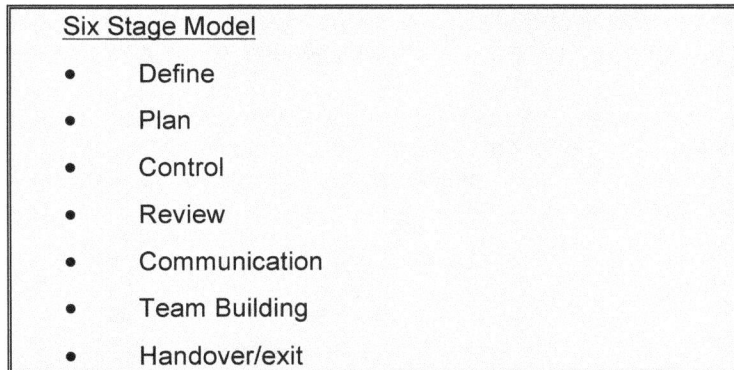

Six Stage Model

- Define

- Plan

- Control

- Review

- Communication

- Team Building

- Handover/exit

OK – there are seven bullet points. At one time review and handover were a single stage, and then there would have been six bullet points. Over time these two have split into separate stages, but the name stuck. It's still a good model, whatever the name, and it gives you a structure on which to hang your processes and techniques. It gives you pointers to what you need to look for at particular stages of the project. It also reminds you of what's to come so you can be prepared.

Another model is the project life cycle. This model has essentially the same elements, they're just called something different and the emphasis is slightly different. The basics are the same.

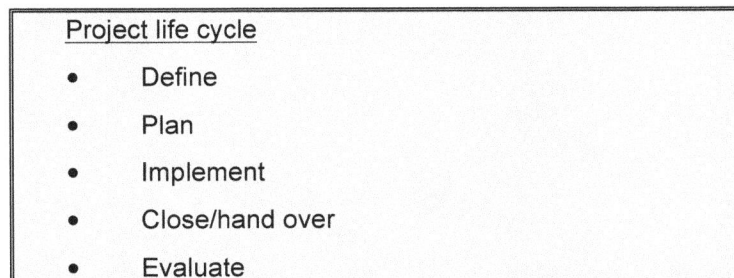

Project life cycle

- Define

- Plan

- Implement

- Close/hand over

- Evaluate

And, of course, there's the PRINCE2 model. This has become the standard model for public sector project management and is rapidly extending its influence to the third sector. It is a very comprehensive model and can be successfully used for small and large projects. In this method, each project management process is specified with its key inputs and outputs and with specific goals and activities to be carried out. The techniques and processes in this book are compatible with PRINCE2.

Each project manager has his/her favourite. I like the six stage model, as I find it useful. It's up to you to find one with which you are comfortable and stick with it.

Using this book

This book presents defining and planning a project as a linear operation. In real life it is far from that. In order to define the project you need to do some planning, scheduling and budgeting. And when you've done that you might need to review the objectives, which means you have to go back to the planning again, and so on.

In order to make this book easier to read, the process is presented as a 'left-to-right' process. When you get to your first draft plan & budget, test it, try to pull it apart, and go through the cycle again. What you get the second time around will be a lot more robust and will be more likely to work.

There are some questions scattered throughout the book and some exercise blanks in the appendices. If it helps you can break from time to time and consider how the points in the book apply to your project(s). You can download blank exercise forms from the website[3] if you don't want to write in the book.

---

[3] www.3rdsectorskills.com

Six Stage Model

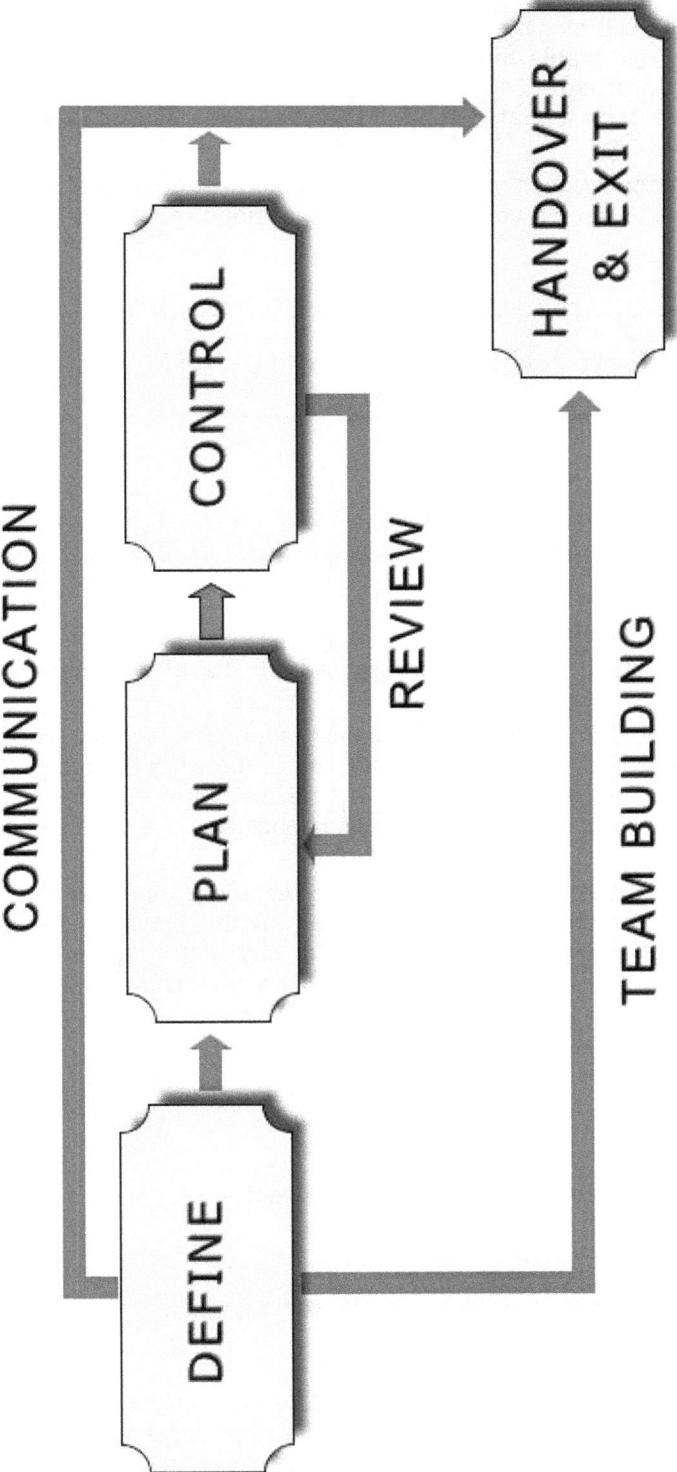

STAGE: DEFINE - Defining your project

The first stage we consider is the definition stage. Here, the project moves from an idea in someone's mind to something tangible. The purpose of this stage is to deliver a document, the project brief, which will enable the project sponsor(s) to make an informed decision about whether or not to proceed. This is a crucial stage. This is the time when the real thinking and planning are done and at the end of this stage the decision to proceed (or not) is taken.

If you treat this stage seriously, then you give yourself the best chance of success. If you skimp on this stage, you're setting yourself up to fail. Spend more time rather than less here.

> *Fail to plan – plan to fail*

So what you have to do here is to

- identify the key objectives of the project;
- establish costs, timescales, resources, deliverables;
- identify measures of success.

You might also carry out a feasibility study.

The deliverable from this stage is the *project brief*, a "must-have" document that specifies what you will be doing in this project.

A project brief contains all the information the project sponsor needs so s/he can decide whether or not to go ahead with the project. It tells him or her what the project is all about, who is affected by it, who is running it, how it will be run, what the objectives are, etc. There's an example of the sorts of topics that should be included in a project brief later on in this book on page 29.

This document is vital. It'll help you keep your sanity as you go through the project and, more importantly from the organisation's point of view, it is the repository of all the project knowledge. Should you fall under a bus, or win the lottery and leave, another project manager should be able to pick up your project brief and carry on with the project.

Note that there are a variety of names for this document. Some call it the *project initiation document*, or the *project specification*. The name is not really important. What counts is what's in the document.

--- ☆ ☆ ☆ ---

Let's make a start on our journey through the life of a project.

A project is born

Projects tend to follow a three step gestation. Not all projects make it all the way through.

Emergence

A need develops, somehow, at some time. It can be a gradual thing or something that happens at a specific moment in time. For example, the 'need' for a website might become apparent over time, as your trustees realise that everyone else has one and your organisation might be losing out because you don't. Or perhaps your organisation has been considering opening a drop-in centre for some time and one day you find you've been left a house in just the right area – instant project!

Recognition

As the need emerges, people develop a gut feeling that something needs to be done to satisfy that need. Perhaps a change in legislation is affecting a large number of your client group, and the need they have is growing. Someone starts to follow up that gut feeling with some solid research. Is the gut feeling right or wrong? Is the perceived problem really the issue or is it merely the symptom of another issue? Which issue should you address?

It's during this stage that you should ask the **really important question:** "Is this project something our organisation should be contemplating?". The project may be a great idea but, if it doesn't fit with the ethos of your organisation, perhaps you should not go any further with it. Assuming it passes the test, then…

Articulation

Now the problem starts to take shape and the goals of the project start to become clear. The stakeholders are identified and their needs are clarified. The problem is now understood and we're starting to think about an appropriate way of solving it. We are starting to define the objectives for the project-to-be. And now we can start to put the project together.

At this stage we have a reasonable idea of what the project is all about. It's a good time to go back to the originator of the idea (if you can) and check that you're on the right track. If you're happy with your progress so far, it's time to start getting more specific, to tie things down a little more.

Project Objectives

Every project needs objectives. They define what it is going to achieve. And there's only one thing worse than no objectives, and that's woolly objectives. If your project is to succeed, you need SMART objectives:

- Specific
- Measurable
- Achievable/Agreed
- Realistic
- Timely

Why bother with all this? Because, if your objectives are SMART, then there can be no doubt whatsoever about them. You can be sure you have achieved them (or not). This is good for you as you can garnish your CV with good solid examples. It's also good for the organisation. If you are going for funding for a new project, then having SMART objectives shows funders that you know what you're talking about. I have seen funding bids with woolly objectives that were simply binned. They might have been great projects but they could not explain clearly what the funders would get for their money. These bids ended up in the round wicker file.

What does it mean to have a SMART objective? Let's consider an example we can all probably relate to! Let us assume it is the New Year and I am depressed about the amount of weight I've put on over the Christmas festivities. I resolve to do something about it. I state my objective.

I'm going to lose weight

This sounds good (and sadly it's an "objective" that can be heard all over the country during January) but it's an awful objective. It doesn't hit ANY of the SMART buttons. Try again.

I will lose 1 stone by the end of next week

This isn't much better. It's specific, measurable and timely, but realistic? Unless I undergo surgery to remove a limb, it's unlikely I will lose that much that quickly. Try again.

I will lose 26 pounds over the next 13 weeks,
so that I will weigh 12st by 31st May

This is much better. It's specific (26 pounds in 13 weeks), measurable (target is 12st and the scales don't lie!), achievable (2lbs per week is what Weight Watchers recommend), but is it realistic? Well possibly, unless you're a true-born Irishman; Saint Patrick's day is right in the middle of this diet and it is just not possible to do without a Guinness or four in the middle of March. So to make the objective more realistic, let's allow a bit of a slip around March 17 and go for....

I will lose 26 pounds over the next 15 weeks,
so that I will weigh 12st by 15th June

Now that's an objective I can live with!

The problem of realistic

This is probably the hardest of the SMART tags to figure out. What does it mean in real life? Well, suppose you have a great project and you reckon you can achieve your objectives, if you devote all your time to it. But is it realistic to expect this? You work for a charity, so I'm betting you don't have a lot of spare time. If you take all your other work into account, can you still achieve all those objectives? (This is similar to the St Patrick's Day problem I've just talked about). Now, get realistic. How much of your time can you devote to this new project? Go back and re-evaluate the objectives.

It's about time for a break – take some time and have a think about your projects, at work or at home. Try to put the project objectives into SMART format. When you've finished writing them, go through and tick off each of the letters SMART to make sure you've hit them all. If you wish, you can use the template at the back of this book, or download a copy[4].

It's not that easy sometimes, but don't be discouraged. The very act of trying tends to focus the mind on what your project is all about.

Objectives, outcomes and outputs

Voluntary sector projects have outputs and outcomes, and they mean different things. I argue that either (or both) are project objectives, and by using the word objective we get around all the debate about whether we're working towards outcomes or outputs or whatever.

Note that you may very well have project objectives that are neither outputs nor outcomes.

For example, let's take a supported employment scheme. The funder is looking for bodies in jobs. (This is a gross simplification, but sufficient for the example.) If you get your

---

[4] From www.3rdsectorskills.com

funding based on how many people you can get into employment, then getting the right number of people in jobs is a project objective.

So, too, is getting the procedures sorted out, the preliminary interviews, recruiting the job coaches, etc. These are essential project objectives but you probably don't get paid for them.

It's essential to have clarity in the objectives of any project. If you are managing a project which relies on outside funders you need to be very clear from the outset what the fundable outcomes are and how you are going to demonstrate achievement of those outcomes. You need to get your funder to agree to your definitions and the method(s) by which you will measure success. Then when the time comes there can (hopefully) be no query on whether or not you have achieved the agreed objectives.

Getting to an objective

From the head of a museum to her project manager. "I want to see more children through the door".

How do you turn that into an objective? How about "We will achieve a 5% increase in the number of children into the museum in the next 3 months"?

Sounds pretty good but it assumes you know how many children are coming through now. How are you going to do it? Is 5% reasonable? Why not 10%?

When you're setting objectives I'm sure you will come across this sort of issue - 5%, 10%, why not 15%? At some stage you just have to use your best judgement and go for it.

If part of the objective is an educated guess, make sure you say so in your project brief. And also make sure you review the objective fairly soon in the project lifespan. You may need to revise it and the earlier you review it, the better.

Are your objectives right?

At the start of this book, I mentioned that projects are about something new and as such, there's a lot of new stuff associated with them. So you're not going to get all your objectives right.

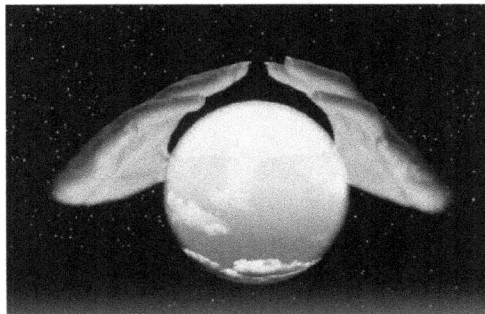

The SMART parts of your objectives at this stage are your best estimate of how things will turn out. It's useful to have a crystal ball, but if you can't find yours right now, you just have to use your best judgment. Don't be afraid to be bold. But be prepared to review your objectives as you go through the project.

A final thought on objectives

So far we have been really picky about getting objectives tied down and making sure they're realistic and achievable. For any project, it's essential to know what you're up against and tying down the objectives is a very good start.

Sometimes, however, you need to say "To heck with it!" and just go with the idea. I'm going to leave you with that thought until page 31. For now, trust me, and work through the rest of the define stage.

> *The greater danger for most of us is not that our aim is too high and we miss it. But that it is too low... and we reach it.*
>
> *Michelangelo*

People in projects

Projects involve people. People do the work and in the third sector people are very often at the heart of what we're trying to deliver. Before we go much further we need to consider the people who are going to be involved in our project.

Stakeholders

An academic definition of a stakeholder is *'any group or individual who can affect or is affected by the achievement of the firm's objectives'* [5] If you replace 'firm' with 'project' you get a definition that works for a project. Sometimes it's not at all obvious who is a stakeholder in a project. But it's important to figure out who they are because they can have a big effect on your project.

Some examples of stakeholders are

- Sponsor

    This is the person or group who set up the project, authorised the resources and gave you the job to make it happen. The sponsor wants the project to succeed. They will help to shape and define the project, publicly support it, and ultimately sign off the acceptance.

- Project Manager

    The person who is tasked with managing the project. That's you!

- Project Team

    The group of people who are going to carry out the tasks and activities of the project.

- External suppliers

    People who supply goods and/or services on which the project's implementation depends. For a voluntary organisation, you might consider funders as external suppliers.

- Internal/external customers

    People for whom the project is being conducted, e.g. clients, service users, etc. If you're working in a large organisation, it can sometimes be useful to consider other parts of your organisation as internal customers.

- Individuals/Groups

    Those who are going to be affected by the project and its outcomes. This could include your client group, members of the public, local businesses, trustees and/or employees of your organisation, etc.

- Project Steering Board

    A project may have a steering board, comprising a group of stakeholders and/or representatives of key business functions who are affected by the project. In the third sector a project steering board will often have client representatives on it. Typically, the board members are senior people with authority to make decisions.

---

[5] (Freeman, R. E. (1984) *Strategic Management: A Stakeholder Approach*, Pitman Publishing, Marshfield, MA).

You can see that there are a wide range of people and/or organisations that can be stakeholders in your project. Looking at the list above you can see that they can exert a great deal of influence on your project.

Stakeholders can make or break your project.

Generally stakeholders want your project to succeed but don't assume that this is always true. Local businesses may well be stakeholders and they might not be so keen on changes to or loss of their customer base; they may well try to scupper you. Even stakeholders whom you believe are friendly may have hidden agendas. You need to understand them because that will help when they make decisions that might otherwise surprise you. You need to manage them throughout the project so that they support you.

Time for some more coffee. Take some time now to brainstorm ideally with your team (and/or others) to think who are the stakeholders for your project. It's useful to make a list of these in a stakeholder register, and note the name of the stakeholder and his/her/their views on the project, and how you will manage them. Like the risk and issue registers it's sensible to review the stakeholder register from time to time to make sure that it's up to date.

--- ☆ ☆ ☆ ---

Let's move on to consider a particular group of stakeholders – the people who will do the work.

Project Team

A project involves people with a mix of skills, maybe from across your organisation, maybe involving people from outside it. This means that you, the project manager and therefore the leader, have to manage people who don't report to you, from different disciplines, possibly from different sites.

But you are a team. You share the goals to get the job done.

This is where a project differs greatly from an on-going enterprise. An on-going enterprise has objectives and targets and outputs, all those good things. But the skills for the scheme usually come from within the enterprise and the objectives tend to be on-going.

In a small organisation the team may be very small and each member may have several hats. But it's still worth thinking about the concept. If you're managing a large project then you'll certainly have to think carefully about your team, how you will manage and motivate them, and how you will monitor their progress.

Clearly you need to populate the team with the right skills to deliver the project. But in order for the team to function well as a team your people need to have the right mix of personal characteristics as well. You need someone who's good with details to ensure you don't miss anything; you need someone who can be a creative problem solver, etc.

There's a lot more about teams and team building later in the book, on page 66 to be precise. For now we just note that it's important to get the right mix of skills.

Considering the options

Feasibility

Depending on the size of the project you might carry out some sort of feasibility study before doing any detailed planning and implementation. It may be that the funders require you to do so before they release the full funding for your project; or it may be that the project is so large that the first stage has to be a pilot scheme. But even if you don't do a full study, you should at least consider the following points before you commit to the project.

- Financial

  Compare the cost of resourcing the project against the benefits it might bring and the cost of not doing it. Ask yourself if it's really worth doing the project at all. What are the implications to the organisation's cashflow? This is very important. It's no good if the project bankrupts the organisation, no matter how good it is!

- Technical

  Will the new system work with the old one? This is particularly true of IT projects. It's all very well replacing your fundraising database but if the new package doesn't easily interface to your membership database then you might well have a massive amount of work to import all your existing data. Is it worth it? If you're working in disaster relief, does your kit all work off the right voltage?

- Environmental and Social

  What are the environmental and local social impacts of this project? Will your new day centre create unacceptable levels of traffic? Do you need to do a disability awareness exercise in the local community before you open your new scheme? With increasing focus on carbon footprints, does your new project still make sense?

- Managerial

  What are the implications for work practices, staff training, etc? Do you have the capacity to take this project on? Do you have the skills? How long will it take to acquire the skills and how much will it cost?

- Value related

  Does this project fit in with the organisation's overall strategy? Does it sit well with the organisation's values? (Think of the very public debates about charities and ethical banking)

  If the project cannot be fully funded, do you wish to put your own money into it because it fulfils your organisation's aims?

Opportunities and Threats

Running a project can bring real opportunities to an organisation but it can also threaten it. If your project is to improve an existing service, you might need to consider the effects your project might have on that service while it's being implemented. A classic example of this is the traffic chaos that exists while an extra lane is being added to a motorway.

Another example is an office move. How will you maintain your operation while your existing office is being packed up and relocated?

Costs and benefits

In business there are (sometimes) clear decisions about the benefits of running a project. If the benefit does not outweigh the cost, there is little point in making the investment. There are well tried techniques for working out the potential benefits.

For a voluntary organisation it is not so clear. It is sometimes worth doing something that will cost the organisation money because it furthers the objectives of the organisation and stakeholders view it as a worthwhile investment of time and money. This is all very good but it makes it difficult to justify proceeding with a project, and even harder to justify not proceeding with a project.

Cost/Benefit example

A local organisation ran a supported employment service which put people with disabilities into real jobs. The service rarely broke even and every year at budget time the trustees were faced with propping up this service with unrestricted funds (which, as we all know, are not easy to get hold of). It was usually a few thousand pounds short on a budget of £100,000 p.a. The trustees invariably agreed to fund the shortfall for three reasons.

Firstly, the intangible benefits of disability awareness amongst the employees of the companies they worked with and the general public that interacted with the companies.

Secondly, the way the project raised the profile of the organisation and the cause.

Thirdly, the self esteem that the service users gained from having a proper job.

The decision to update a payroll system, for example, can be evaluated on purely commercial terms. But the decision to open a drop-in centre is another thing entirely. How do you measure the benefit to the organisation, to its clients, to its funders? You have to find some way of quantifying the benefit because, even if you have a fantastic project, it is just not worth doing if it is going to bring the organisation down.

But no matter how you judge the 'good' of a project, you still need to know the financial impact it will have on your organisation. We'll look at how to assess this later, starting on page 60.

Putting the cost/benefit analysis together

The input to these calculations comes from the consideration of many factors, such as:

- What resources will we require and what will they cost the organisation? Don't forget to include management time and not just the costs of the project team.
- What product will be produced, in what quantity and of what quality? (In this context product can mean something your organisation produces to sell, or a product in terms of clients, say, number of clients re-housed, or with jobs, etc.)
- How much can we charge users if the charges are to cover costs? (Indeed, can we charge users at all? Another way of looking at this question is, how much do we need to charge the funder to cover the costs?)

- What cost savings will we enjoy or what fines/penalties will we avoid by implementing the project?
- What are the development costs?
- What are the operational costs? Getting the project completed is one thing, but what are the on-going costs of running the scheme you've just set up? Now is a good time to know this information, before you kick off the project!
- Are there tangible benefits? What are they? Can you quantify them?
- Are there intangible benefits? What are they and how can they be expressed?
- What are the implications for cash flow? (Remember: cash flow is king).

All of these factors need to be considered when judging if the benefits of doing the project outweigh the costs. Although very important, money is not the only factor to take into account when putting the cost/benefit analysis together.

Discounted cash flow

If the project budget is large and/or it will take a long time to complete, then it may be a good idea to do a more in-depth financial analysis and take into account the way that the value of money changes over time. If this applies to your project, take some time to read Appendix 2 which goes into this topic in some detail.

Risks

Risk and contingency planning

Projects are necessarily risky – you're doing something new and/or producing something new, and that is a risky business. As a project manager you have to manage the risk to your project by taking whatever steps are necessary to minimise any impact of any risk on your project.

You must plan for risk and be specific about it. Think of all the things that could possibly go wrong and figure out what to do if they happen.

Write it down. This is one time when you need paperwork. Construct a risk register where you write down each risk, analyse it to see how likely it is, consider the impact if it happens and then plan your way around it.

Let's look at risk in more detail.

What is risk?

When voluntary organisations talk about risk they usually think of things like risk assessments for activities, protection of vulnerable people, etc. That's not the sort of risk we're talking about here.

Here we are talking about *risk to the project*. Basically, you need to look at anything that could affect your project adversely. Consider anything that will upset your project balance – things that could affect the budget, the timescale and/or the scope. Think about anything that will prevent you from meeting your project objectives. For example, if you are managing a project to deliver a service to vulnerable people, a risk to the project could be "what happens if we have an incident involving a vulnerable person?". Will the project have to stop? What are the financial implications to the organisation if it does?

Project risks

Most risks to a project come in the following categories. It's important to consider them all as you may find thinking about a category suddenly produces a risk you weren't aware of before.

- Physical

    This covers such incidents as loss or damage to information, equipment, or buildings as a result of an accident, fire, theft or natural disaster. What happens if your PC is lost or stolen or your client database goes up in smoke? (And you with the annual return still to do...) What happens if the day centre is vandalised or burns down? How and where will you operate your service after a disaster such as this?

- Technical

    Here, consider systems that don't work or don't work well enough to deliver the anticipated benefits. A computer crash could be one of these, or a payroll system that doesn't work properly. Suppose your project was to implement a new fundraising database. A major risk here is getting the old data (all those hundreds of names and addresses) from the old system to the new. Can it be done automatically?

    A technical risk doesn't have to be a computer – what happens if you're on overseas relief work where the power supply is 110V and your kit works off 240V?

- Labour

    If key people become unable to contribute to the project, it could have a big impact on your project. This could be because of illness, a career change, industrial action or a win on the national lottery, for example. A syndicate win on the lottery, I suggest, would have much more impact than an individual win. Fortunately it's not that likely, but worth thinking about, just in case. It could be you!

- Political/social

    What would happen if support for the project is withdrawn as a result of change of government (national or local), a policy change by senior management in your own organisation, protests from the community, adverse media coverage, complaints or action from current or potential service users, etc?

    Think carefully about how your project will be seen by government back-benchers, local councillors, press, media and voters.

- Liability

    This type of risk includes legal action (or threat of it) because some aspect of the project is thought to be illegal or the possibility of compensation claims if something goes wrong. We live in a compensation culture now so you really have to think hard about this one.

- Fiscal risk

    Government has a habit of defining financial obligations before becoming committed to a course of action and not providing projects with unlimited financial guarantees, either in law or in fact. There are a number of examples of government initiatives that were welcomed by the third sector, and implemented with a will. Then someone noticed that the spend was exceeding their expectations, and the back-pedalling started.

Where would you put the incident involving a vulnerable person discussed in the previous page? There's a fiscal risk if the project is stopped as a result of the incident. There's a liability if an injury is involved. There's the reputation of your organisation, which I would argue comes under political/social. So, one incident throws up risks in all sorts of ways, and they all need to be considered.

Impact analysis

It's not good enough to talk about risk in a woolly way. You need to have some way of weighting risk so that you concentrate on the right areas.

To start with, list everything that might go wrong with your project, no matter how daft it may sound right now. This exercise is best done with your project team because if they are going to be doing the work, they probably have a better idea of some of the risks than you do. Get the team together with a large piece of paper and a pen, and get brainstorming. At this stage, consider anything.

Having written your list, consider the likelihood of each risk actually happening. Then assess the impact on the project (or organisation) if the risk happened.

Assign a low, medium or high value to the risk of each thing happening, and then a value to the impact it would have if it actually happened, again using low, medium and high. You can then construct a table like the one in Figure 3 and assign each risk to one of the boxes. When you're deciding which box to use you might also want to consider how far away in time the risk is. For example, many voluntary organisations might put "change of national government" as a risk. Many projects depend on political support which can change with a change in administration. The probability of this risk occurring will be different depending on how long it is since the last general election. The political situation will determine the seriousness of the likely impact. The risk assessment is something you'll have to keep up to date, so it's ok to put a serious risk that is a long way off into a less serious box right now, provided you keep the risk register up to date, and allow risks to move between the boxes.

An unusual risk?

At one of my courses an organisation which worked abroad listed the "United States Army" as a risk. This produced some merriment, as you can imagine, but it was a serious issue for this organisation. They were running a project in Afghanistan and the US Army was poised over the nearby hills. The political situation was deteriorating and there was a real possibility of an invasion. This would have a major impact on the project (!) and so the organisation had a contingency plan ready to evacuate their people to a place of (relative) safety, should the tanks start to roll.

The position in the table will help you decide how much urgency with which you will have to address each risk, and the amount of detail you will have to have in your risk management plan.

	Low impact	Medium impact	High impact
High probability			 ⛈
Medium probability			
Low probability			

Really **bad** news!

Figure 3 – Impact table

You can now use this table to come up with a priority list. The most urgent risks to consider are those with the thundercloud. They're likely to occur and they're going to hurt if they do.

Risk Register

Clearly you can't work from this table, it just isn't practical. So it's a good idea to transfer the risk information into a risk register. This is a very important document – a must have – where you write down the risks, how likely they are to happen, what their impact will be, and, most importantly, what you're doing to minimise them. A risk could be described in many ways and it's very easy to get confused so I strongly advocate numbering each risk so that there cannot be any doubt about what it is, and insist on always using the number to identify it. In this way there is no excuse for confusion.

So here I've numbered the risks simply 1 and 2. You may be tempted to use H1 and M1 to differentiate between high and medium risks, but if you change the priorities of a risk this approach can get confusing.

Review the risk register often; at the very least, review it at every project review meeting.

Risk no	Description	Impact	Probability	Action
1	Drop-in centre building will not be ready in time for opening day	High	Medium	Weekly meetings with contractor. Keep opening day provisional. Schedule 'official opening' for one month after actual (contingency)
2	Furniture storage required, but not yet identified.	Medium	Low	Pursue volunteer's lock-up. Keep one month's rental of commercial garage in budget.
3				
4				

Figure 4 – Risk Register

Time for another break.

This time think about the possible risks to your project. Take the worst possible scenarios and write them down. And then use your judgment to assign probabilities and impact to them all. Remember it's just your judgement at this stage.

Again, you can use the template at the back of this book, or download a copy[6] if you need more space.

In the next section we're going to see what we can do to mitigate the risks you've just listed.

Strategies for dealing with risk

What sorts of actions can you take to minimise risk? Risk management experts reckon there are only 5 different strategies you can adopt.

- Prevention

    Terminate the risk - prevent it happening. If it's possible you might consider doing things differently to prevent the risk happening at all or stop it having an impact on your organisation if it does happen. A good example is a voluntary

---

[6] From www.3rdsectorskills.com

organisation looking at taking over a local authority service but having to deal with the TUPE issues of pension schemes. The financial risks are often huge and several voluntary organisations have prevented the risk by walking away from such a project.

- Reduction

  Take action to control the risk in some way. Either reduce the likelihood of it happening or limit its impact to acceptable levels. A good example here is fitting a sprinkler system to a building. You are reducing the likelihood of a fire taking hold by dumping water on it at an early stage, but also if it does take hold you are lessening the impact by keeping it (a bit) under control until the fire brigade arrive.

  On the flip side, you need to weigh the impact of fire damage against the impact of all that water.

- Transference

  Pass the management of the risk to a third party in such a way that the impact of the risk is less of an issue for the project. An example might be taking out weather insurance on an outdoor event. If the event is rained off you should recover your costs from the insurer. However, you won't be able to recover lost publicity because the 10,000 people you were expecting to turn up decided to stay at home in the dry.

- Acceptance

  If there's nothing you can do about the risk without incurring unreasonable costs, you have to accept the risk. You might be reliant on a single employee for some key skill. The risk here is, if that employee leaves, the skill will leave with him/her. It's usually not practical to employ a backup person, so you do what you can to ensure that the knowledge of that employee is captured within the organisation. But you have to accept that when s/he leaves, it is going to be difficult for a while.

  If you're organising an outdoor event, and insurance is prohibitively expensive, you may just have to take the chance and accept that it might rain on you.

- Contingency

  This strategy involves 'Plan B', where you have some planned actions ready to put into place should the risk event happen. A classic example here is a disaster recovery plan. If your building gets flooded or burned down you have a plan to enable you to continue until alternative accommodation can be found.

  Keep your contingency plans up to date. You may want to review these plans in the same way as you review the risk register.

When you are considering the risks to your project remember that taking action to mitigate a risk uses resources, so a consideration must be the cost of mitigating the risk versus the cost if the risk were to materialise. An every day example is if you were to buy, say, a new washing machine. The salesman offers you an extended warranty, to mitigate the risk of your machine failing in the next 3 years. Is it worth the extra cost of the warranty up front, or are you willing to take a chance and pay for a repair IF it is needed?

The biggest risk of all - CHANGE

Without doubt, changes to the project brief after the project has started present the biggest risk to the project. It's also the most likely risk to hit you. And if you are going to manage it you need a process to handle change.

More project management time is spent on managing change than almost any other issue. Change is one of the prime reasons that projects fail. There are numerous examples of projects that are years late and millions of pounds over budget and often it's simply that the project specification was subject to constant change.

An example in the voluntary sector might be the introduction of additional reporting requirements after the contract has been placed. This is a change to the specification and this particular change means more work for your team; work which was not budgeted. If not challenged this could mean your project will fail, e.g. go over budget, take longer or only deliver some of the declared objectives. This sort of change *should* mean the negotiation of an agreed variation to the project objectives with additional money to pay for the extra work.

If your funder is reluctant to pay more, you can either refuse to do the additional work, swallow hard and do it, or pull out of the project. The choice you make is dependent on all sorts of factors. It may be that the additional reporting suits your own purposes and perhaps you will do it anyway for the benefit your organisation will gain. This should not stop you making a fuss about it to the funder. Perhaps you can wring a concession out of them for another project.

The point is, you should not take a change to the specification without a murmur.

Bringing it all together

Project brief

So having done all this thinking and planning you are ready to complete the definition stage. The deliverable from this stage is the *project brief*, also sometimes called the *terms of reference*, *project specification*, *project initiation document*. It's a very important document and every project, however small, should have one. How big it is and how much information is in it is dependent on the size and complexity of the project.

The document needs to contain sufficient detail to enable the stakeholders to make informed decisions. They need to be reassured that all major issues have been considered and that the organisation's resources will be well invested if this project is started.

Contents of a typical project brief

A typical project brief could contain the following. Your organisation may well have other requirements, but the goal of the project brief is to allow informed decisions to be made.

- Background

  Why we are contemplating this project? (Emergence and articulation of the need)

- Project definition

  What this project is all about, what are the objectives (SMART)

- Scope, exclusions and interfaces

  What this project is NOT about – defines the boundaries and where the project fits in to the rest of the organisation/world

- Project organisation structure

  Who is on the team and what their roles and responsibilities are. This helps avoid stuff "falling down the cracks"

- Communication Plan

  How we will ensure that all stakeholders are kept up to date - presentations, reports, website, etc. What will we communicate to whom, how and how often.

- Project Quality Plan

  How we will deliver the product to the required quality standard. This may be a standard organisation document with modifications for this particular project. It includes what tools we will use, what processes, etc.

- Project controls

  How the project will be controlled, how often review meetings will be held, who will attend, what the reporting requirements are (to funders as well as internally), etc.

- Initial Business Case

  Overview of the business case for this project, cost/benefit analysis, cash flow, etc. The business case will be reviewed periodically through the project but you need to establish that there is a good case right at the beginning.

- Customer's quality expectations

  What the customer (whoever it is) is expecting. If this is different from what we are expecting to deliver, how it is different. This could be opening hours for a drop-in centre, or staff/client ratios, etc.

- Acceptance criteria

  How we know we've achieved our objectives. Have these criteria been agreed with the customer/funder, etc?

- Major deliverables

  List of major deliverables from each major stage of the project. This list could include internal deliverables, such as the project specification, as well as the finished items.

- Initial Project Plan

  Top level schedule, key project milestones. There needs to be a balance here between a plan that's detailed enough to give enough information, but not so detailed that it takes massive resource to put together. Remember, there's still a chance at this stage that the project will not go ahead. (NB we haven't talked about planning yet. It's the next section of the book but there needs to be a top level plan included in the project brief so we have a good idea of the timescales and resources required.)

- Initial Risk Log

  First draft of the risk log. This is a living document, so will change throughout the project. At this stage you are looking to convince the person or people who matter that you have considered the risks to the project/organisation. You are giving them information to make a well informed decision on whether or not the project should go ahead.

- Exit Strategy

  What will happen at the end of the project to continue the work it started? If the funding cannot be extended, how will the organisation wind up the project with dignity to itself and the people it supports?

The aim of the project brief is to enable the decision makers in your organisation to make an informed decision on whether or not to give the go-ahead. It should contain enough detail to convince them that you've considered all the options, that there's nothing lurking in the detail that will leap out at some future time and cause them, or you, aggravation.

The project brief as a fund-raiser

If you're bidding for funding, a project brief is a good document to produce. If you get it right, you are presenting your funder with a well thought out, comprehensive document telling them how you will spend their money, and what benefits they'll get out of it. They'll see how you will control the spending of their money, and you will demonstrate that your project represents value to them. It's a great document.

Project kick-off

Often the project brief is presented to the stakeholders at a kick-off meeting where the details of the project are examined and the go/no-go decision is made. Sometimes this meeting is a grand affair attended by lots of people. Sometimes it can be a simple one to one with your boss.

I argue that you should always have a project kick-off. Even if it's just you and a colleague taking an hour in a local coffee shop going through the brief, it's worth it. It gives you the opportunity to look through the document in a detached way and just make sure you've thought of everything and that there are no little (or gaping) holes in your project.

Once you have the go-ahead you should not discard the project brief. It's a great reference book to use throughout the life of the project, to remind you of the project objectives, and the "rules of engagement".

When you come to close the project down, the project brief will also form part of your Portfolio of Success – more on that subject later (page 98).

The "To heck with it" moment

Up until now we've concentrated on being very clinical about the project. We know about the objectives, the budget, the resources required, etc. I've advocated taking a cold, hard look at it all and making a logical decision on whether or not to proceed.

That is absolutely what you must do – 99% of the time.

But now and again a project will appear that just has to be done, no matter what. Do you remember Live Aid? Do you think for a moment that Bob Geldof looked at objectives, budgets, etc. and concluded that the project was a non-starter? Maybe he did, but he still said "To heck with it" (or knowing Sir Bob's reputation, probably something unprintable) and went ahead and did it anyway. And it was a resounding success.

It's a very, very risky strategy, but there are times when you just have to do it. If you've followed the process so far, then at least you will make the decision with the best possible information at hand. You will know the risks and uncertainties.

And once the decision's made, you will still need to plan and monitor and control. So don't give up now. Keep reading!

STAGE: PLAN - Planning your project

In the real world life doesn't work in a nice neat orderly fashion. You can't progress through the define phase without doing any planning. You need at least a top level plan in order to produce the project brief and you'll probably have to re-plan a couple of times before you're happy with the result.

But, in order to make this book readable, it has to be written in an orderly fashion, which is why we're just coming on to planning now.

Let's look at ways to plan. The techniques are equally valid if you're producing a top level plan for the brief or a detailed plan for actually running the project. And once you start implementing the project you will undoubtedly have to re-plan several times as things change. The project plan is a living thing and will change through the life of the project.

> *In preparing for battle I have always found that plans are useless, but planning is indispensable*
>
> *Dwight D Eisenhower*

Where do I start?

There are basically two ways to start planning your project.

You can start by listing the key steps for your project and then see what deliverables drop out of this process. For example, if the project is a one-day workshop, your key steps might include 'Book venue' and 'book speaker'. The deliverables would then be 'venue booked' and 'speaker booked'.

Alternatively you can start with the deliverables ('venue booked' for example) and the key step for this would be 'book venue'.

The end result is the same. How you get there is a matter of style, whatever suits you.

If you're thinking of adopting PRINCE2 as your organisation's model, you should know that it recommends that you start with the deliverables (products in PRINCE2-speak), and then figure out the key steps. This style suits me, and that's the one we're going to use in the rest of this book.

Products/Deliverables

Some project managers use the word product instead of deliverable. In my view the words are interchangeable. It really doesn't matter what you call them as long as everyone in your team understands your definition. For now we'll go with the PRINCE2 word – product.

Products can be physical items like day centres, or handbooks, people in jobs or even project documentation. They can equally be changes in people, say, managers trained in a new process. Products are the changes you are inflicting on the world.

- Some sort of change achieved: someone trained or placed in a job or housed, etc.
- Something produced: a book, a building, a database, etc.

Products are handed over to someone who is authorised to receive them and the handover procedure must be agreed beforehand, preferably in the definition of the product. This is so there is no misunderstanding later on in the project. (If you have a small project the person who accepts the product might be you with one of your other hats on, but nevertheless, thinking in this way even for this sort of situation is a good habit to get into).

Products / outcomes / deliverables and jargon

Is it a product, a deliverable, an outcome or an output? Essentially, all these words are all terms for defining what you are trying to do and how you prove you've done it.

I can't get worked up about which word to use. If your funder wants to call a product an "evidence of achievement" then do just that. Remember that "he who pays the piper calls the tune". Just make absolutely sure the whole team understands what the phrases mean and how you know you will have demonstrated your "evidence of achievement".

How will you know you have achieved it?

You need to have some tangible way to demonstrate that you have achieved your goal. This helps when asking the customer to sign the acceptance note (and the cheque?).

Suppose the project objective was to change the service focus of an organisation. You could define as your product...

> *Evidence that 80 key managers have been trained in managing change.*

But how do you prove it? The managers might have turned up at the course but do they really know how to manage change? Weren't some of them asleep yesterday afternoon? Ticking an attendance sheet shows they were there, not that they learned anything.

A better definition might be to show...

> *Evidence that 80 managers have successfully managed change.*

This might take longer to demonstrate and achieving it might be more difficult, but it's a far better measure of the success of the product.

Goal Displacement

This can happen when you and/or your team get fixated on one particular aspect of the project and lose sight of the big idea. Suppose you're running an employment scheme, whose sole reason for existing is to get your clients into real, long-term jobs. One of your objectives may well be to secure a set number of jobs per year. If you fixate on achieving the numbers you may well be placing candidates in jobs that just aren't right for them. The result is that, although you're winning the numbers game, you have a higher than expected turnover of candidates, a longer waiting list, less value for money for the funder.

It's all too easy to fall into this trap. The answer is to keep re-visiting the project goals. Keep them in mind all the time. Print them out and pin them to your wall, put them in your PDA, Filofax or smartphone. Do whatever you feel is necessary to keep them in front of you and your team all the time.

Don't get distracted from the reason for implementing the project, and you're less likely to suffer from goal displacement.

Identify key steps

Now you know what your products are you can start to work out what you need to do to get them. What are the major tasks that must be achieved and in what order?

Before we go any further we need to define a task.

I define a task as a piece of work that has a beginning and an end (almost a mini-project!). It needs to be self-contained in that it can be done without any outside interference. Some examples are

- Boil an egg
- Address an envelope
- Paint a door

Note that although each of these tasks assumes you have completed certain pre-requisites, (e.g. you have an egg and the means to boil it) they are self-contained. They are the sorts of tasks you can give to someone to do without you having to stand over them. You can also tell when they're complete. Having said that, if you were to give someone the task 'paint a door' you should, of course, also specify which door and what colour you want it painted, and perhaps which paint to use.

In theory you could also define 'decorate a room' as a task because if you have all the pre-requisites you can just get on and do it, but I don't like it because the timescale is a bit long and you can easily split it into smaller items that are themselves tasks.

'Construct publicity campaign' is not a task. There will be things that have to be done and then waiting time whilst the tasks are be completed. For example, 'design poster' could be ok as a task but, before you can distribute your posters, they need to be printed and that's likely to be done by someone else, so that's a task for them and not you.

You need to be sensible when defining a task. It needs to be small enough so it can be completed in a reasonable time frame but not ridiculously small. If you split your project into too many really small tasks then you'll spend all your time keeping track of them and not managing the project.

Although I advocate leaving considerations of resource until after the schedule has been put together, it's sensible to think about the sorts of people who will be doing the work when you split the work into tasks. For example, if you have experienced staff in your kitchen then 'boil an egg' is ok. But if you will be dealing with absolute beginners, then you might want to split this task into smaller ones like 'put cold water into saucepan', 'add egg and bring to boil', 'boil for 4 minutes', etc.

There is no right answer. You need to apply your judgement to the task of splitting the work into tasks.

Duration vs. effort

Tasks *always* have a duration attached to them. Just note that duration isn't the same as effort. It's similar to preparation time and cooking time on a recipe – the effort is the preparation, when you are actively working on the project, and the cooking time is similar to the duration where the task can't complete until some time has elapsed.

Duration vs. Effort - Stuart's mean beef stew

This is the best example of the difference between duration and effort.

Take some beef and chop it into small-ish pieces. Chuck it in a cast iron pan with a little oil and stir around until the bits are brown. Pour in a bottle of your favourite beer (Newcastle Brown or Guinness are particularly good here), bring to the boil, cover and shove in the oven for a few hours.

When it's nearly time to finish, chop some garlic and onions. Fry the onions gently, adding the garlic. Add some tomato puree and flour and cook gently for a couple of minutes. Get the casserole onto the hob and slowly add the tomatoes and flour until the sauce is thick enough. Serve with baked potatoes and vegetables – yummy.

How much effort is involved? About half an hour – 15 minutes to chop the beef and get it ready for the oven, another 15 to finish the dish at the end.

What's the duration of the task? Several hours – you have to start to cook a long time before you want to eat.

If you want the real recipe – you can download it from the website.[7]

The duration of 'print posters' could be quite long. The effort required could be small because this task is likely to be carried out be an outside agency.

What about resources?

Up to now we've been thinking about resources in general. We haven't been thinking about specific people, but we haven't forgotten that we will have to do this at some stage. Just for now, we'll concentrate on figuring out which tasks have to be carried out to create your project's products. We'll consider the resources fully later on when we come to put the plan together.

Top tip

When identifying tasks and scheduling them, always involve the team if at all possible. If you do, then you will benefit from their experiences of actually doing the work. You will benefit from having more than one brain working on the project and at the end, when the plan is put together, you will have the team's buy-in and commitment to achieving what you have worked out together.

---

[7] www.3rdsectorskills.com

Scheduling

With any project it is vital that you understand the relationships between the various tasks and/or activities. This is particularly important with larger projects when there's too much information to keep in your head.

What follows is equally applicable to large and small projects. We'll go through how to build up a project plan. Lots of the stuff that follows is done for you when you use a software package but it is important that you understand the principles so that you can see when the software is lying to you. It happens. On several occasions I have carefully input all my activities and dependencies and when I looked at the completed output it was clearly wildly out. It was only by going through the project in detail that I found a couple of errors, corrected them, and then got something more like real life.

As we go through the process some parts might seem a little strange. The reasoning is that you should impose as few restrictions as you possibly can on your first plan because sure as eggs is eggs, you will have to change it, and if you plan this way you'll find it easier to change.

As Publilius Syrus said in the first century BC...

> *It's a bad plan that admits no modification*
>
> *Publilius Syrus*

...so it makes sense to build a schedule that can be easily modified.

Putting a project plan together is simply taking all the tasks and assembling them into the right order. Then you assign the appropriate resource to each task (human, object, cost). Then you work out the total time for the project to run, add up all the costs, and you're done!

Simple!

Starting off – the salami technique

A salami is a large object, too large to eat at one sitting. So a good way to approach it would be to cut it up into meal-sized pieces and store them appropriately. When it came to a meal, you could take a single chunk and then slice that into bite-sized pieces. You can now eat. And over time you will eat the whole salami.

So it is with projects. The salami technique is all about breaking a project down into bite-sized pieces which makes the whole thing possible.

To start off, break the project into manageable chunks. At this stage think 'high level'. So although I said previously that 'construct publicity campaign' is not a task, that sort of thing is good enough for the first pass.

Once you have a list of large chunks just take a moment to make sure that it's complete. Apply the acid test.

Check you're not assuming any steps that have not been written down. They may be obvious to you now but when the project is underway there's a real chance that if the task isn't written down it won't happen, so check again. If you pass the acid test then you can go on to the next job which is to take your large chunks and link them together, showing the dependencies between them.

Once you're happy with this then take the large chunks and break them down further. Repeat the process until you have tasks that are small enough to assign to your project team as self-contained units. At each stage, apply the acid test to make sure nothing falls down a crack.

How far do you go?

The big question is how far do you break down the project? And there is no good answer – it's a matter of judgement. It depends on so much. For example, if I wanted breakfast of tea, toast and a boiled egg, that amount of detail would be enough for my daughter to implement the project successfully. However, my son doesn't know how to boil an egg, so I'd have to break that task down further in order for him to do the same thing.

You need to have the slices of salami thin enough so that the people who are working on your project can eat them successfully without much input from you, but not so thin that you're spending all your time feeding them.

So when breaking the project down you need to be mindful of the calibre of staff you have or are likely to have, so you can slice the salami accordingly. But enough of this metaphor...

Now you have a list of tasks, you need to link them together and when you've done that you will have your schedule. But just before we do that, let's look at how projects can be represented diagrammatically, because that will make linking a little easier.

How to represent the project

Now is a good time to introduce the concept of logic or network diagrams. That's a fancy name for a diagram showing how the tasks are linked. Project managers are simple souls and we love pictures. Pictures are much better than words at showing how the project hangs together and what the dependencies are. Project managers' favourite pictures are almost always either PERT charts or GANNT charts.

PERT charts

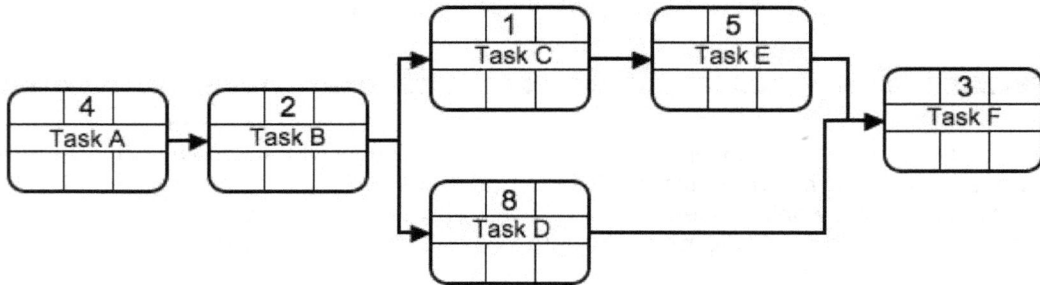

Figure 5 – PERT chart

PERT (Programme Evaluation and Review Technique) charts were first used in the 1950s by the US Navy Polaris project and they show in a pictorial manner the flow of work through a project.

Figure 5 shows a PERT chart of a simple project. The tasks are represented by boxes with the name of the task across the middle. The number at the top tells you the duration of the task. All the other little boxes have meaning, too, and we'll come to them in a few pages (Figure 15 on page 47). The arrows show how the tasks are linked together. In this diagram task B can start only when task A has completed. Tasks C & D can't start until task B has complete, but then tasks C & E are not dependent on task D, so they can run in parallel with it. Finally task F can't start until both of tasks D & E have completed. We'll use this sort of diagram in a few pages time to do something exciting. Don't flip the pages, be patient.

PERT charts give you a clear view of the flow of the project. It's easy to see what the dependencies are and where the bottlenecks are happening. But it's almost impossible to see what should be happening when because there's no obvious link to time on this diagram.

Another down side is that PERT charts take a lot of space to see what is happening. If you've got a large project then you had better invest either in a local forest or a powerful magnifying glass!

Gannt charts

GANNT charts (named after Henry L Gannt, who invented them in the 1920s) are the (probably) more familiar bar charts that show tasks and timescales. They are graphical, with a calendar along the horizontal axis, and the tasks appearing as bars. It's not so easy to spot the dependencies between tasks but it is easy to see what's supposed to be happening when. You just scan down the chart at the appropriate date and if there's a bar there then that task should be happening.

You can also see when your peak workload is; it's when there are the greatest number of bars in parallel crossing your chart.

Figure 6 shows a Gannt chart of the same project that we had in Figure 5.

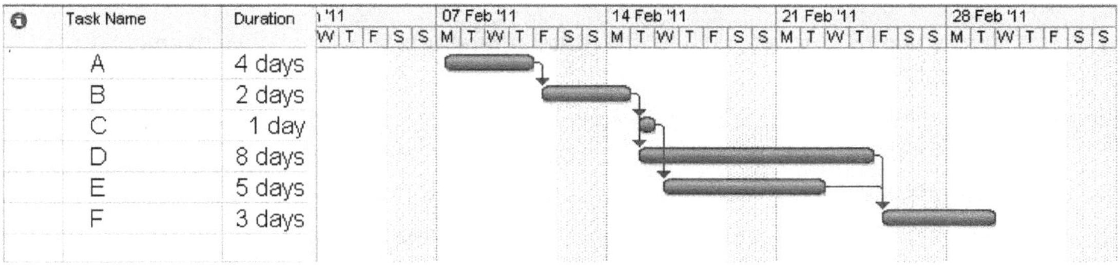

❶	Task Name	Duration
	A	4 days
	B	2 days
	C	1 day
	D	8 days
	E	5 days
	F	3 days

Figure 6 – Gannt chart

It's more intuitive and it's fairly easy to see what's supposed to be happening today. For example if you look at Friday 11 Feb, you can easily see that task B is supposed to be happening. But if there are a lot of tasks and the diagram extends over more than one page it gets tricky to spot the connecting arrows.

Gannt charts are more economical on paper when you print the plans, provided you format them sensibly. In Appendix 3 you will find a Gannt chart and a PERT chart for the same project, so you can compare the two diagrams. I had to split the PERT in two so the text would be big enough to read.

Linking tasks

We've just seen tasks linked together. Let's think about all the ways in which tasks can be linked. In project management there are three different types of link you will come across.

Finish - Start | This is the most common sort of link. The task cannot start until its predecessor completes;
e.g. you can't use the pen until you have taken the lid off.

Start – Start | This link indicates that two tasks can start together. Sometimes the link can have a duration attached to it, showing that one task can start at some time after the other – this is called the lead time; e.g. you can start the task of putting the Christmas cards into the envelopes once your partner has written the first one – there is a lead time of 'one card'.

Finish – Finish | This link is used when there are two tasks that can be carried out in parallel, but one of them cannot finish until the other one has completed;
e.g. suppose Joe is writing the Christmas cards, and Mary is writing the envelopes and putting the cards into them. Both tasks can happen in parallel, but Mary can't finish her task until Joe writes the final card.

Examples

It's very important to be very clear about dependencies. It is only the task that is dependent, not who is working on it. Let me give you an example.

My car is parked off the road behind a locked gate. In order to drive away I need to complete three tasks

- open the gate
- start the car
- drive away.

(I have conveniently ignored closing the gate afterwards – I want this example to be as simple as possible.)

In this simple example the dependencies are as follows

- I cannot drive away until the gate is opened – finish/start
- I cannot drive away until the car is started – finish/start
- Opening the gates and starting the car are independent tasks. It does not matter which I do first.

If I am alone, then either starting the car or opening the gates will come first but this is a decision I can make at the time. One day it may be frosty so I will start the car first to allow it to warm up whilst I'm opening the gates. Another day I will choose to open the gates first. I can make my decision based on the circumstances at the time. One day, I may have someone else with me and the tasks can be performed simultaneously. For the initial plan, however, I will ignore the resources I may or may not have.

This is a fairly trivial example but it is important. When your project is big and complex you must not impose dependencies that don't really exist. If you do, you may well end up restricting your freedom of action unnecessarily.

Just think: life is bad enough, you don't have to make it worse by putting unnecessary restrictions on yourself (cheerful thought for the day)!

Overlapping tasks

We will use start/start and finish/finish links when tasks run in parallel. For example, suppose you are laying some pipes in the street. A Gannt chart of the first draft programme could look like the one in Figure 7.

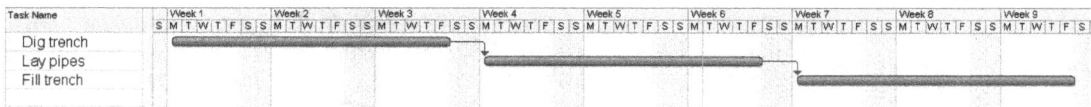

Figure 7 – Laying pipes: first draft

All the links are finish-start so the arrows go from the end of one task to the start of the next.

But there is no need to wait until the whole trench has been dug to start laying the pipes and similarly you don't need to wait until all the pipes are laid before you can start filling in the trench.

So you might allow the trench diggers a week before you start laying the pipes and similarly for filling in. Figure 8 shows the modified project plan.

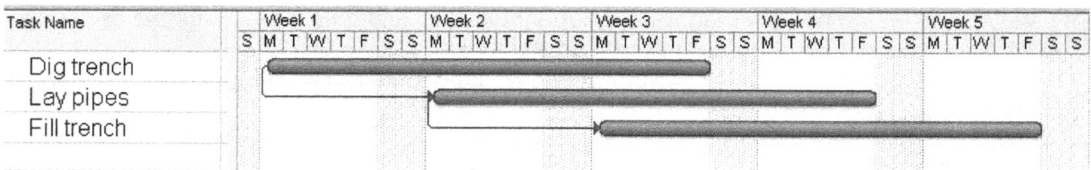

Figure 8 – Laying pipes: second draft

(Note how the arrows show the start-start link going from the start of one task to the start of the next)

- The task 'lay pipes' can start one week after the digging starts. Digging leads it by one week.
- The task 'fill trench' can start one week after the pipe laying starts.
- The task 'lay pipes' cannot complete until one week after the 'dig trench' completes so there is a week's lag in there; similarly with the 'fill trench' task.

It's important not to forget the lag times because if laying the pipes takes longer than planned, the trench filling task will also slip.

The net result of this overlap is that a project that was originally scheduled for 9 weeks could be completed in 5. This is good news all round, especially for the local residents! At this stage we haven't considered any resource constraints, so the 5 week schedule may have to alter. We'll look at the impact of resources a little later on. For now, we just note that theoretically, this project could complete in 5 weeks.

This example is pretty straightforward but it illustrates that you have to think carefully about dependencies. Don't put a finish-start link in just because it's the default value. And don't put any artificial constraints such as assuming that Joe will be doing tasks F to K, so they'll have to be finish-starts because we've only got one Joe. It may end up like that but if you put those constraints in from the beginning you are reducing your flexibility and you may end up with a non-optimal project plan. It is really best to be as flexible as possible at this stage – there is plenty of time for reality to upset you later on; put that off as long as possible. Also the more flexible you are now, the easier it is for any software you may use to work to your best advantage.

Putting the schedule together

So back to your project. You have your list of tasks and you need to link them together. My suggestion for this job is to take a pad of Post-Its, a white board and white board pen. Write a brief description of each task on a post-it and stick it to the board. Once all the tasks are there you can draw lines on the board to link them indicating the order in which they must happen and any dependencies. You're constructing a PERT chart with Post-Its and pen.

It's probably easier to do the Post-It and white board routine in the same way that you produced the list of tasks, that is, start with the top level and then increase the detail level by level until you have a complete chart or set of charts.

The reason for the Post-Its and white board is that it is easy to make changes. It's easy to move tasks around and change the links. Keep on refining your diagram until you are happy with the result. Then take a photograph of the board with a digital camera and transfer your plan to paper or a computer without losing anything. It's much easier to transpose to another medium this way than to have some poor soul frantically scribbling in a notebook with pencil and rubber as you chop and change the plan.

Once you have your set of charts you have your first draft plan. It won't be worth very much in its current state as we don't know who's doing what yet. It can all change when you consider the resources for each task/activity. We'll do that later. But at this stage you have the dependencies and you are part way towards an initial idea of the duration of the project.

(If you use software don't panic about transferring your stickies plan to the computer. All you have to do is put in each task and duration and make sure the links are right, and the software will do the rest for you.)

How long will it take?

Having produced the network the next stage is to figure out how long the plan will take.

Start and Finish Times

When you build your network you will find that some tasks attract spare time.

Let's consider another very simple example. You want to make egg and toast for breakfast. An egg takes 4 minutes to cook and a piece of toast takes 2 minutes. Note that the two tasks are independent but eating breakfast is dependent on both the toast and egg tasks being complete.

Here's a network diagram of this project

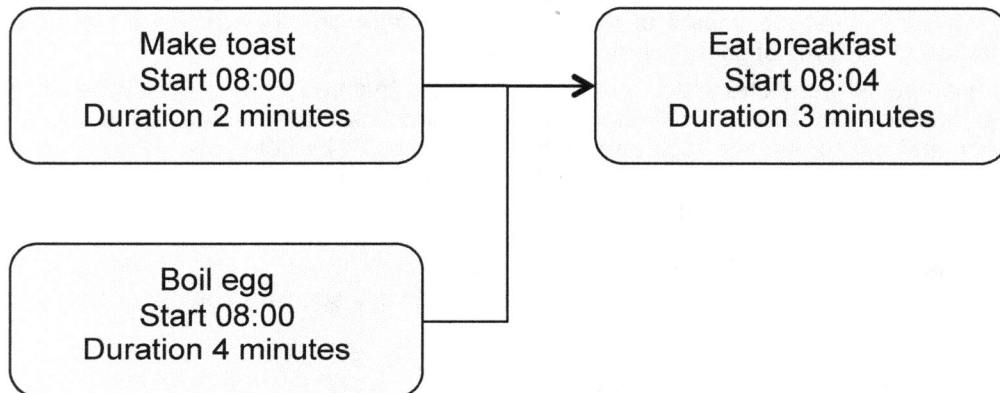

Figure 9 – Breakfast: network diagram

You start to cook breakfast at 08:00 and you put the egg on to boil and start the toast. The egg takes four minutes to boil but the toast is ready after only two minutes. What a rotten start to the day! The toast is cold by the time the egg is ready. The task 'make toast' has some spare time associated with it.

This is a good example of *float*. Because 'eat breakfast' is dependent on both the egg and toast, and the egg takes 2 minutes longer to cook 'make toast' has two minutes float, which is project management speak for spare time. You could delay the start of the toast by 2 minutes and breakfast would still be on time and what's more, the toast would still be warm – a result!

So we see that each task has two (potentially) different start and end times. These are

Early Start	The earliest possible time at which the activity can start
Early Finish	The earliest possible time at which the activity can finish
Late Start	The latest possible time at which the activity can start and not impact the programme
Late Finish	The latest possible time at which the activity can finish and not impact the programme

Going back to breakfast the early start for boiling the egg is 08:00 and the early finish is 08:04. The late start is also 08:00 because if you started it any later breakfast would be late. Similarly, the late finish is 08:04. This is an example of a task with *zero float*.

It's different for the toast. You could start the toast at 8:00 but you could put off starting until 8:02 and the toast would still be ready on time. The early start for the toast is therefore 8:00 and the late start is 8:02. Early finish is 8:02 and late finish is 8:04.

This is a Gannt chart for the same project. Note that the float is much easier to see on this diagram.

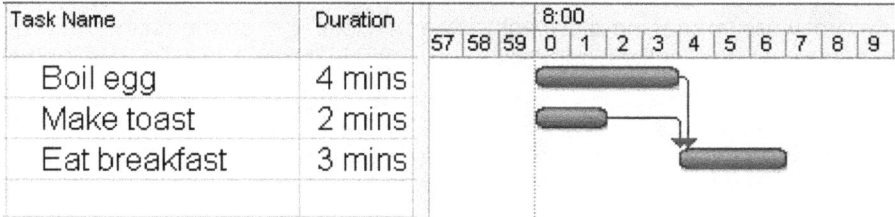

Figure 10 – Breakfast: Gannt chart

This example also nicely illustrates another type of dependency. Up until now we have assumed that any task will be undertaken *as soon as possible*. This is generally true but in the case of cooking the toast we would be better off starting this task *as late as possible*. If you use software to construct your schedule you will come across an option for each task to decide which of these two should apply. Remember, however, that scheduling a task for as late as possible means there is no scope for things going wrong. There's no float.

Let's make life a little more complicated and add the task 'butter toast' to our little project. This task will take one minute

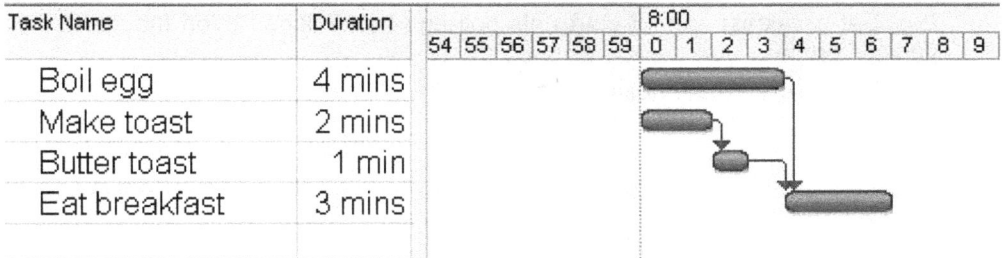

Figure 11 – Breakfast – add 'butter toast'

If you delay making the toast by 1 minute then buttering it is also delayed. Both 'make toast' and 'butter toast' share the same 1 minute float. In this case we say that the two tasks have a *total float* of 1 minute but 'make toast' shares its float with 'butter toast'.

If 'make toast' is not delayed then 'butter toast' has all the float and because this float can be used up without affecting any other task (e.g. boil egg) it is called *free float*.

The names of the float aren't really important. The way they work together is.

Critical Path

Two of the tasks in our breakfast project have no float at all. If you don't start the toast at 8:00 you won't delay "eat breakfast" and therefore the whole project. But if you don't start the egg on time you will. And eating the breakfast must happen on time for the project to complete on time. So cooking the egg and eating breakfast are tasks which must happen on time if the project is to complete on time. From this we get the definition of critical path.

> The critical path is that list of dependent tasks where a delay in any one task will cause a delay to the whole project.

It's clearly vital when managing a project to keep a close eye on the critical path because as soon as a task on the critical path slips your whole project will be late unless you do something about it.

A good rule of thumb is to adopt the Pareto 80/20[8] rule to the critical path. 80% of your grief will come from the critical path so spend 80% of your time worrying about it, but save 20% to keep an eye on everything else. Not a foolproof or absolute rule, but worth keeping at the back of your mind.

Finding the critical path

There is a straightforward method to work out the critical path.

1. Plot a diagram of the tasks/activities and their dependencies. This diagram is referred to as the network for pretty obvious reasons.

2. Make sure it's right.

3. Go through the network writing down the early start date for each task/activity. If you come to an activity that depends on more than one predecessor then the early start is the *latest* of the possible start dates.

   E.g. Eat breakfast cannot start until boil egg has finished even though make toast finishes earlier.

   Here's our very simple network again.

---

[8] The Pareto principle (also known as the 80-20 rule) states that for many events 80% of the effects comes from 20% of the causes. Business management thinker Joseph M. Juran suggested the principle and named it after Italian economist Vilfredo Pareto, who observed in 1906 that 80% of income in Italy went to 20% of the population. It is a common rule of thumb in business; e.g., "80% of your sales come from 20% of your clients." It also applies to a variety of more mundane matters: we wear our 20% most favoured clothes about 80% of the time, we spend 80% of the time with 20% of our acquaintances, etc.

In the project management context, I suggest that 80% of your headaches will come from 20% of the tasks in your plan, and they're likely to be the ones on the critical path.

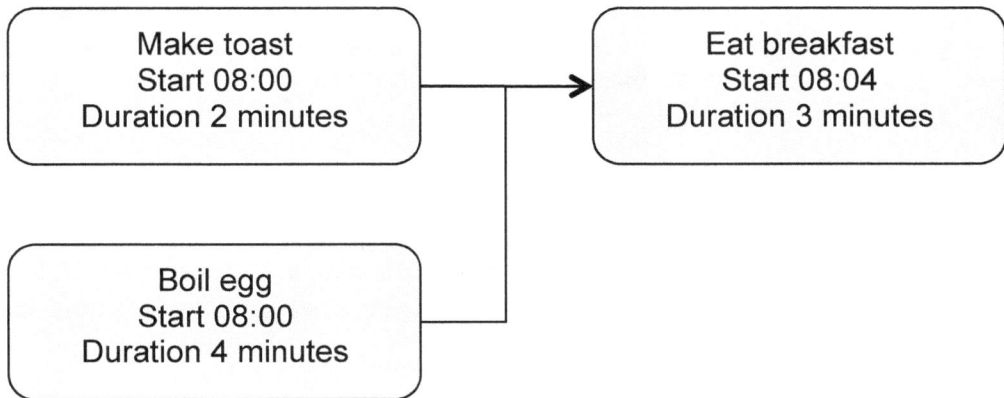

Figure 12 – Breakfast: network diagram

By the time you've got to the end of the network you know how long the whole project will take. In this simple case the answer is 7 minutes; 4 to cook the egg and 3 to eat breakfast. You may question the fact that you spend 4 minutes making breakfast and only 3 eating it, but by the time you get to eat you're late for the train and have to rush!

4. Now to find the critical path start at the end of the project and work backwards, working out the late start for each task/activity. The critical path is given by those tasks where the early start and late start times are the same, i.e. there is no *float*.

    This example is really easy. It's clear just by looking at the diagram that the critical path comprises 'boil egg' and 'eat breakfast'. These tasks are highlighted in bold in the diagram.

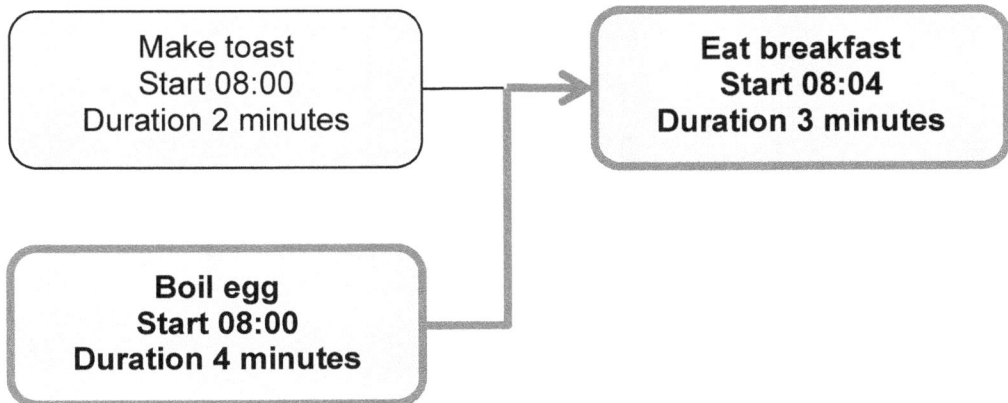

Figure 13 – Breakfast: critical path

So to recap. The critical path is the path (or paths) through a network where there is *no float*. *Any* delay in *any* of these tasks will impact the end date. Note also that you now know the minimum duration of your project. It's the total time taken to go along the critical path.

As a project manager the critical path is the path that demands your attention.

But beware; it does not take much for the critical path to change. In our simple example suppose there is no fresh bread and you have to take some out of the freezer. Toasting frozen bread takes 5 minutes, not 2. Suddenly your network has changed. Toast is on the critical path and your project will run 1 minute longer because of that. Boiling the egg is no longer critical - you have 1 minute of float on that task.

--- ☆ ☆ ☆ ---

Critical path analysis - worked example

That was too easy. Under normal circumstances we can't just look at the diagram and see the critical path. Let's look at a more realistic example and work out the critical path for it.

We will start by getting out yellow stickies out. On each sticky note we need the following information

- Task name
- Duration

That's all for now. We will fill in the rest of it as we go through the exercise. By the time we've finished we will have added

- Early start
- Late start
- Early finish
- Late finish

And in addition we will know the theoretical minimum duration for the whole project and we will easily see the critical path.

At this point we would normally head for the whiteboard but to coin a phrase, here is one I prepared earlier. Imagine we have had the brainstorming session, covered the whiteboard with stickies and pen and this is the result. Note that all the links are finish-start (that's most likely what you'll have in real life, too)

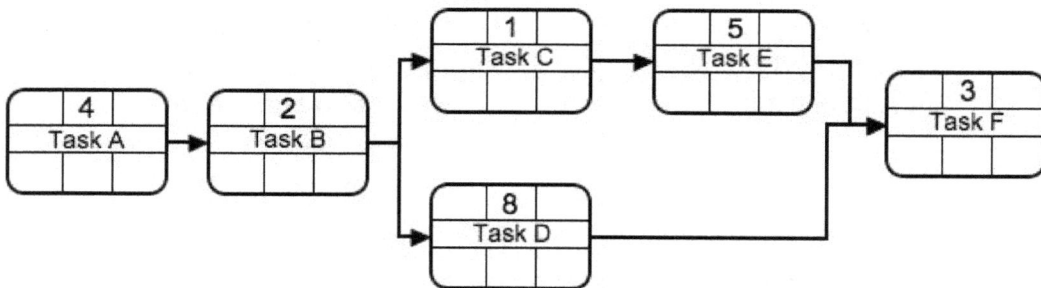

Figure 14 – CPA: first stage

Before we start, let's just pause to understand the layout of the little boxes. Each box represents a task, and contains within it all the information you need to put your network together.

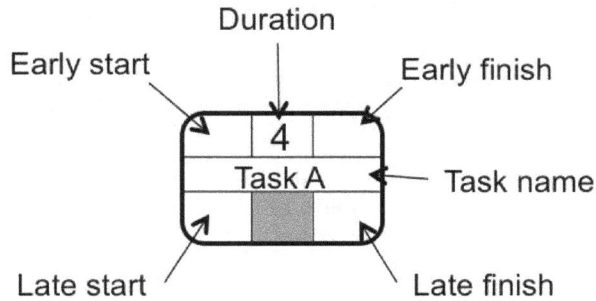

Figure 15 – Network diagram node

The little grey box is spare at this stage. You can use it later to mark off completed tasks for example.

We're going to go through the network and fill in the boxes. We'll start at the beginning of the project.

Look at task A. It is the first task in the project and so the project starts when task A starts. We can fill in the early start date for this task and it's zero. The network now looks like Figure 16.

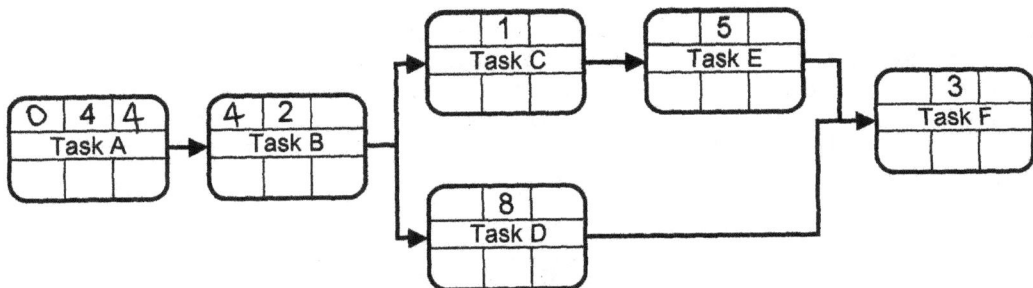

Figure 16 – CPA: time for tasks A & B added

Why zero? Why not one?

Suppose we're going to start this task on Monday, which we'll call day 1. It's a 4 day task so that will take us up to Thursday night. Then the next task can start on day 5 which is Friday.

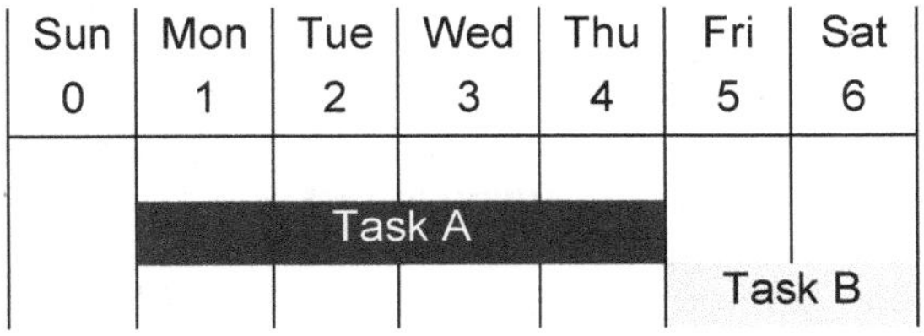

Sun	Mon	Tue	Wed	Thu	Fri	Sat
0	1	2	3	4	5	6
			Task A			
					Task B	

Figure 17 – End and start times

If we imagine that task A starts at the very end of Sunday (midnight, say), putting a zero in the top left box makes sense. When you add the duration of 4 days to it (0+4=4), then putting 4 in the early finish box signifies that you've finished the task at the end of day 4. It gives a clear link between the number of days a task takes and the calendar. You know that if task A has a finish date of day 4, then on the fourth day of the project you should see task A wrapping up.

Let's move on. Look at the link between tasks A & B. It's a finish-start which means you can start task B only when task A has been completed. And if task A completes at the end of day 4 then we can logically put the end of day 4 as the early start of task B.

It's the same kind of logic that allows you to fill up your day with back-to-back meetings. No-one thinks twice about one meeting finishing at 11:00 and the next starting immediately, at 11:00. We're using the same sort of logic here.

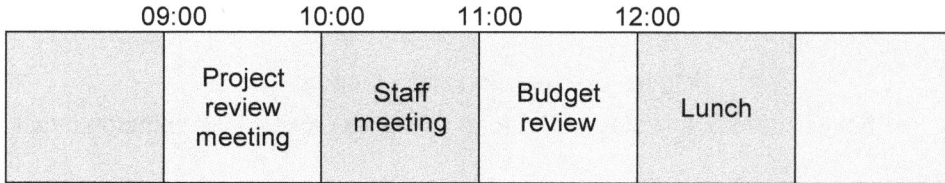

Figure 18 – Back to back meetings

So we put the start time for task B as the same as the end time for task A – day 4. Now add the duration of 2 days for task B and we can see that it finishes at the end of day 6, which is Saturday, which makes absolute sense.

Now it looks as though we have a problem. The network splits after task B and both tasks C and D are dependent on ask B. Relax, it's not a problem really. We know that task B completes at the end of day 6 so the earliest task C can start is also the end of day 6 because it's a finish-start link. So the number 6 goes in the top left box for C. And because the link from B to D is the same, a finish-start, the early start for task D is also 6 – see Figure 19.

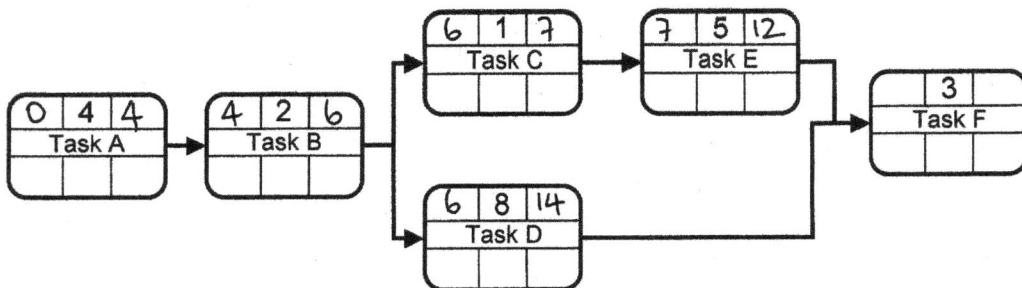

Figure 19 – CPA: third stage

Work along the network and the next problem-ette comes when we think about the final task F. What's the earliest it can start? According to task E it can start on day 12 but according to task D it's 14. Since F cannot start until *both* D and E are complete its early start has to be 14. Now we know the start date we add the duration of F and we get an early finish of 17. We have completed the forward pass and we know that the theoretical minimum duration for the whole project is 17 days - Figure 20.

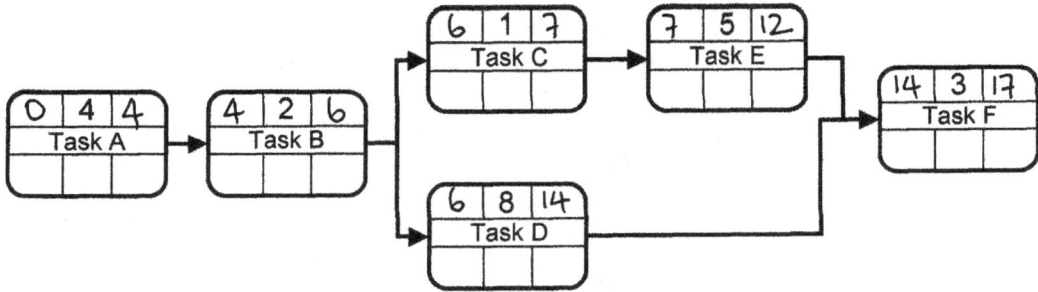

Figure 20 – CPA: Forward pass completed

That's all very well but there are a lot of empty boxes and we still don't know what the critical path is. (Well, we do because it's obvious, but we're going to pretend we don't so we can get the general technique.)

So now we have to do the *reverse pass* and start from the end and work backwards.

We know that the end of the project, which is the finish time for task F, is day 17. This is therefore the late finish for task F, so we can fill in 17 in the bottom right box and because the duration of the task is 3 days the late start must be day 14 (17-3=14) – see Figure 21.

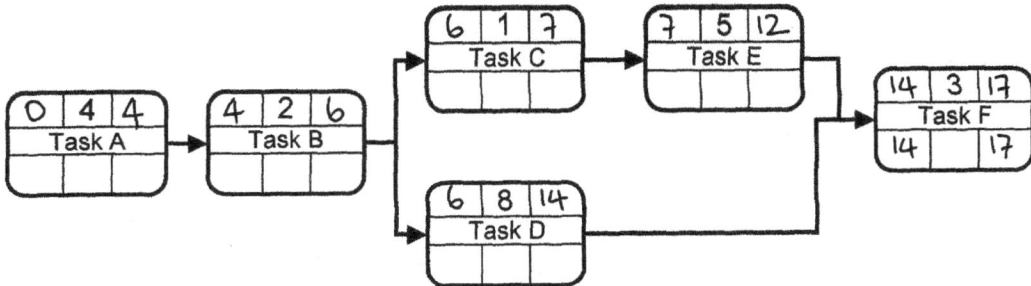

Figure 21 – CPA: starting reverse pass

Straightaway we have a small problem to solve. If the latest F can start is day 14, what's the latest that both D and E can finish? Clearly it's day 14. Even though E can finish on day 12 it doesn't *need* to finish until day 14.

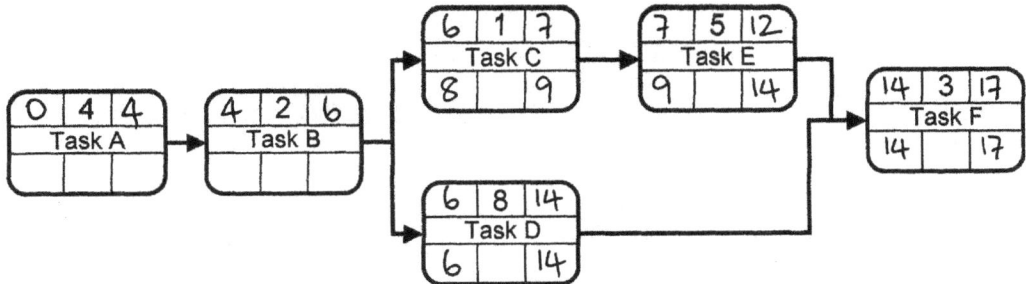

Figure 22 – CPA: sixth stage

We carry on towards the left of the diagram taking away the durations from the late finishes to get the late starts until we get to task B. Both C and D are on finish-start links from B so

49

the latest that B can finish has to be the earlier of the late starts for C and D – i.e. day 6. It can't have a late finish of day 8 because by then task D will be late.

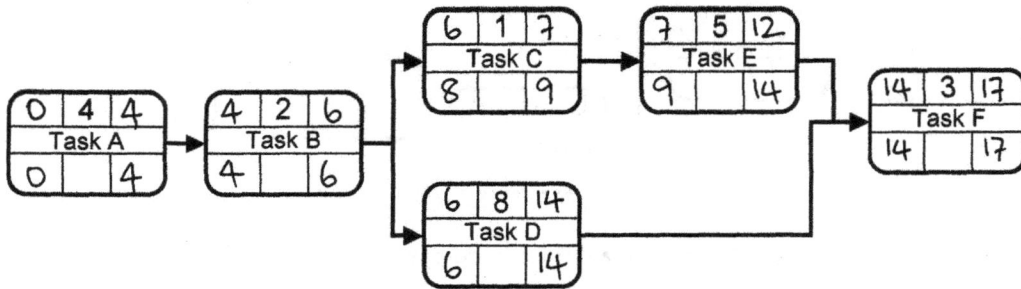

Figure 23 – CPA: reverse pass complete

So in goes number 6 in the bottom right of task B and moving towards the left we find that the late start for task A is day 0. This is a relief because it would be a mighty strange project if the starting task had some float!

Now look at the boxes in Figure 23 and spot which tasks have the same early and late starts and early and late finishes. There is no float at all here which means that if any of these task run late then the whole project will run late, and that's the definition of critical path.

The critical path is the path comprising tasks A – B – D – F.

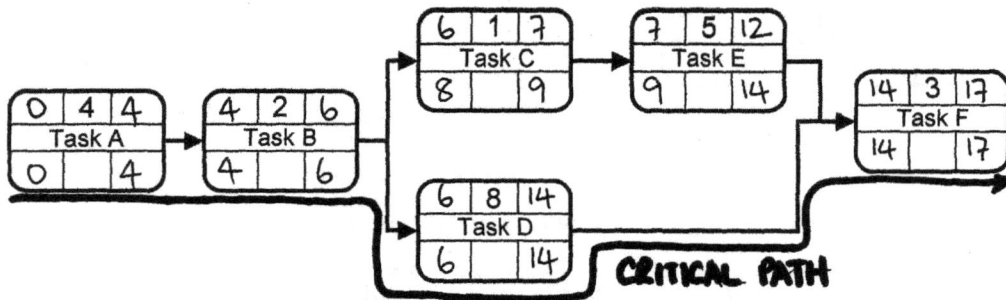

Figure 24 – CPA: complete with critical path

I will repeat what I said earlier. Be very careful. Tasks C & E are not on the critical path but ignore them at your peril. There's only 2 days float in there and it doesn't take much to lose a couple of days. You need to look very carefully at the critical path (80%) but you must, must, *must* keep an eye on the non-critical items as well (20%).

Further exercise: if you're feeling brave (or bored) there's another exercise at the back of the book (Appendix 1) with a more complex network diagram. The answers are in Appendix 5, just to stop you peeking too soon.

If you're doing a small project you might do this sort of thing by hand. But if you decide to dance with the devil and use a computer, the project management software will do all this for you. It uses the same techniques but does it a whole lot faster.

Once you have your network, check it at least twice to make sure you have ALL the tasks in, that they are in the right order, that the dependencies are correct and that the links are correct.

We now have found the theoretical minimum time to complete the project and the critical path. The chances are it still bears little relation to reality because we haven't thought who is going to do the work and any resources they're going to need. It's time to add these to the plan.

Resources

So far, we have carefully ignored resource and there's a reason for this. If you assign resources too early in the process, it's very easy to inadvertently add constraints. This will lead you to construct a plan that will restrict your flexibility later on. For example, if you assume that you need Joe for certain tasks it will alter the way you put your plan together. It may be that further down the line you decide that Mary can do some of those tasks. But if you've already assigned them to Joe, it will be harder to adjust your plan to re-assign them to Mary. It is much easier to adapt your plan if you add the resources after you have your schedule.

My advice is to forget all about resources when you put your initial plan together, just concentrate on getting the tasks and the dependencies right. Once you have your network correct then you can allocate resources. That's why we've left it until now.

Adding resources to a schedule

When you add resource, you add people and things to the project. If it's obvious who will do the work, add them as a name. If you don't know at the moment then put in sensible descriptors, like 'fund raiser 1' or 'family worker'. You can always change the names later.

Note that resources can be things as well as people. A machine, a conference room and a minibus are examples of things that can be considered as resources that need to be assigned to your project.

If you're assigning people as resources, remember not to assign them for 100% of their time. If you do, you are fooling yourself. Even with the best will in the world, no-one will devote themselves 100% to any task. You need to allow for sickness, holiday, working on other tasks, etc. And for resources like a minibus you need to allow time off for getting its MOT, a service, etc. You can plan these as 'holidays' for the resource.

Although it looks as though you are adding unnecessary time to your project, you are, in fact, putting together a more reasonable plan, and one that you have a much better chance of achieving. A good rule of thumb is only to assign 80% of a person who is in theory working 100% on your task. You need to reduce this percentage correspondingly for people who are assigned to you on a part-time basis.

It doesn't fit!

Once you've assigned your resources, you will almost certainly notice that you are in trouble – you'll probably have a situation like your one fund raiser doing 17 day's work all on the same day. No matter how wonderful or hard working he or she is, this can't happen. It is, alas, another nasty dose of realism!

Levelling

What you need to do now is to 'level' the plan. This is where you smooth out the humps and hollows in your resource usage. Simply put, you move the tasks around so that you are using your available resource in a sensible way and try to keep all of your team gainfully employed every day.

The bad news is that once you've levelled, you will usually find that now your project is going to take a whole lot longer than the first pass suggested. Sorry, that's life!

There are two sorts of levelling, depending on which type of constraint is the most restrictive.

Resource-limited levelling

This technique works by assuming you have a fixed amount of resource and cannot change it. You modify the plan so that the known level of resource is never exceeded. Almost always this means either accepting a later completion date than you predicted when you assumed every task would start on its early start date, or accepting that you can't do all the things you wanted to.

An example of this might be preparing a mail shot. It would be nice to get it out by the end of the month, but if it slips into the following month it's not the end of the world. No-one outside the organisation knows, so there's no embarrassment. You could accept a slip, or maybe go with less content.

Time-limited levelling

This is far more common! This is where you keep to the original timescale and fiddle with the resources. A good example of this is a Valentine's Day Grand Ball. It's not a lot of use if it's held in the first week of March. No, this project absolutely has to complete on February 14th. If you are going to hit your schedule you have to get more resource into the project or do less. (This is going back to the quality/scope discussion right at the beginning of the book.) You may have to accept and work with resource overloads, pull people off other work to help out, mobilise some volunteers, etc in order to complete the project in the required timescale.

In commercial organisations the management can sometimes throw money at a project and employ lots of extra people to complete the project[9]. (This doesn't always work, of course, but management hardly ever remember this fact when the situation comes up.) If you are running out of time and have the luxury of having extra resource available, then get that resource in as early as you can. You will need extra management time to manage them, you may need time to train them, you will certainly need time to bring them into the project team, and none of this extra time will be in your original project plan.

Realistic levelling

In practice, what works is a combination of time and resource limited levelling, and if that doesn't solve the problem, then you have to resort to some scope modification. Perhaps you can de-scope the project so that there is less to do. Perhaps you can move some of your

---

[9] *The mythical man-month*

This is the title of (quite a heavy) book about project management which concentrates on software engineering. The theme from which the title is drawn bears exposure here, as it is relevant to all sorts of projects. [The Mythical Man-month: Frederick P. Brooks, Jr, pub: Addison Wesley 1995, ISBN 0-201-83595-9]

It is very common for software projects to slip. And just as common is the senior management reaction – "Throw resource at it!" The perception is that if you are 2 man-months behind schedule, then adding 2 people to the team will fix the problem in a month!

This is a fallacy. Often adding even one more member of staff puts a project further behind, as some of your existing resource has to be diverted to train the new person. A well-established rule of thumb is that you should allow a good 3-4 months on a complex project before a new person, however good, would be contributing fully to the project.

I mention this because the same sort of thing applies to any project. If it is getting behind, you can't just throw resource at it (even if you can afford to) and expect the timescale to recover. It just won't happen! What you can do, only if you start early enough, is to plan to introduce additional resource (if you have any) in a controlled way. Unfortunately authorisation to add resource usually comes at the panic stage when it is too late.

resource around a little or maybe change the order of some of the tasks. It could be that you end up doing some things less efficiently than you could do but making better use of your resource long-term. Think of this as the credit card solution. It is less financially efficient to buy, say, a washing machine, with a credit card and pay it off over six months. But if yours is broken and you need a new one *now* and you can't afford to buy it with cash, you may be prepared to accept the additional cost in return for the convenience.

What is important is that you make your management aware of the limitations on your project. It is no good going to them well into the project and telling them you're going to be late because you don't have enough resource. Frankly, it's usually fairly pointless telling them at the start of the project, but if you do, then at least you can feel more comfortable with yourself. And you never know, they may find more resource or offer suggestions to help!

Warning

One common situation that arises is where a project is subjected to time-limited scheduling and no heed is paid to the resource implications this throws up. Virtually every organisation on the planet is resource limited so it really makes no sense to blindly assume that you can find all you need to complete your project on time, no matter what. Yet this is a very common belief amongst senior management.

A very useful output from a time-limited scheduling operation is an indication of just how much resource you would need to complete the project in the time allowed. It is possible to use this information to try to bring a sense of reality to your senior management or trustees. You can use your plan to show them, for example, that in order to complete the project as specified in the required time you need 5 full-time workers. If you only have 3, then they really cannot expect you to deliver on time unless they extend the project timescale, reduce the requirements, or give you more resource. One final thought on this subject – working through the planning like this gives you solid data to enable you to objectively demonstrate the truth to the outside world.

If you don't have spare resource, then it's back to balancing the Scope/Budget/Time triangle and you have to start getting creative.

An example of levelling

Let's look at an example. This project is my family getting out of the house in the morning. I've picked this because I reckon everyone can relate to this 'project', and the principles it illustrates are absolutely transferable to any project.

Some background: there are five of us in the family with only one bathroom. We all need to get out at about 07:45. Because I go to work and drive past Susan's school I give her a lift, so we need to leave together. Mary (my wife) drives to work past the boys' school so she gives a lift to John and Paul, so they need to leave together.

The tasks for each of us are 'shower', 'eat breakfast' and 'get dressed'. There are a couple of zero time tasks which are 'get up' and 'ready to leave'. The zero time tasks are milestones and are useful to mark the beginning and end of each person's series of tasks. The two girls have an extra task each, which is 'dry hair'. This is a pragmatic reflection of how life is in our house.

I started the plan by working out the dependencies for these tasks and assigning a time to each of them. I then constructed a Gannt chart to show the project (Figure 25). I made one small change. Although my wife and I get up at the same time, she goes for breakfast while I have a shower. Apart from this small difference all the sets of tasks are in the same order.

I assigned resources to each task, both human and non-human (the bathroom). The tasks in the Gannt chart are labelled with the resources required.

The final links at the right side of the lists of tasks show who leaves with whom, with a milestone (the black diamond shape) for the departure time of the two cars.

Figure 25 is the first attempt at the plan. The following illustrations were generated using Microsoft Project 2007.

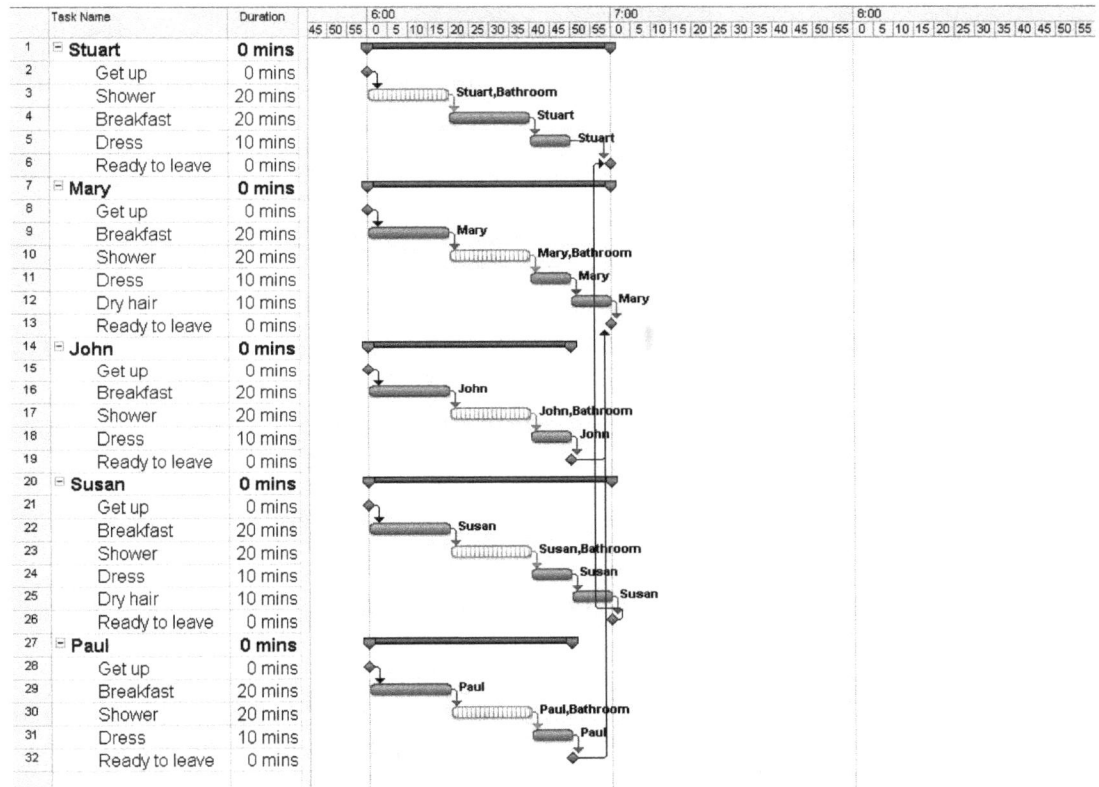

Figure 25 – Levelling: stage one

This is a pretty good first stab. It only takes an hour for us all to get ready. But there's a resource issue. 4 out of the 5 of us need to share the bathroom at the same time. I'm okay because I use it while everyone else is having breakfast. Sharing the bathroom is an option but it's not practical even if they were that way inclined – it's far too small! So we need to do something about it. The obvious solution is to level the plan on resources. The bathroom is well over-used as a resource, so let's level its use. It's possible to do this by hand but I've used the software to do the work for me. Figure 26 shows what happens when the software has levelled on resource. It has gone through the tasks in order and where it found a conflict it's moved the 'lower' task to the right. The only exception to this is that it put Susan in the bathroom earlier than the boys because I told the software to give her priority over the boys. Empirical data shows she takes longer after her shower to get ready despite what the project plan shows.

	Task Name	Duration
1	⊟ **Stuart**	**0 mins**
2	Get up	0 mins
3	Shower	20 mins
4	Breakfast	20 mins
5	Dress	10 mins
6	Ready to leave	0 mins
7	⊟ **Mary**	**0 mins**
8	Get up	0 mins
9	Breakfast	20 mins
10	Shower	20 mins
11	Dress	10 mins
12	Dry hair	10 mins
13	Ready to leave	0 mins
14	⊟ **John**	**0 mins**
15	Get up	0 mins
16	Breakfast	20 mins
17	Shower	20 mins
18	Dress	10 mins
19	Ready to leave	0 mins
20	⊟ **Susan**	**0 mins**
21	Get up	0 mins
22	Breakfast	20 mins
23	Shower	20 mins
24	Dress	10 mins
25	Dry hair	10 mins
26	Ready to leave	0 mins
27	⊟ **Paul**	**0 mins**
28	Get up	0 mins
29	Breakfast	20 mins
30	Shower	20 mins
31	Dress	10 mins
32	Ready to leave	0 mins

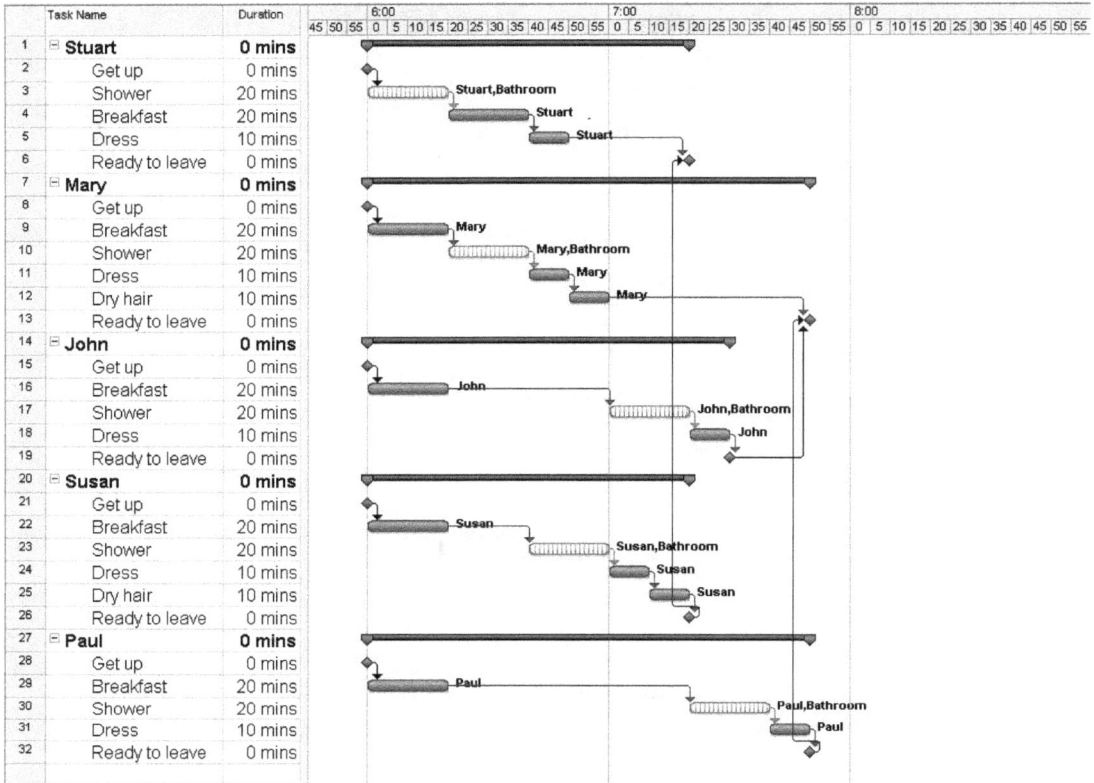

Figure 26 – Levelling: stage two

The first thing to notice is that the plan now takes a lot longer. Because the bathroom is required by everybody, the project timescale has almost doubled. We now can't leave until 07:45. This would normally be a major problem for a project, but in this particular case it's not such a big issue. 07:45 is an acceptable departure time because if we leave then we can all get to work/school on time.

The second thing to notice is that the children are getting up much earlier than they need to. If we follow this plan they'll be up early and then spend a good deal of time sitting around waiting. Have you ever tried to get teenagers to get out of bed one minute earlier than they need to? Can't be done.

So let's think again. Let's change the way the tasks are scheduled. If we accept that we are going to leave at 07:45 we could schedule the children's tasks to start as late as possible rather than the default 'as early as possible'. This would allow them to stay in bed longer, but we would eat up all our slack. In effect, all the children's tasks would become critical.

Again letting the software do the work we get the version of the plan in Figure 27.

56

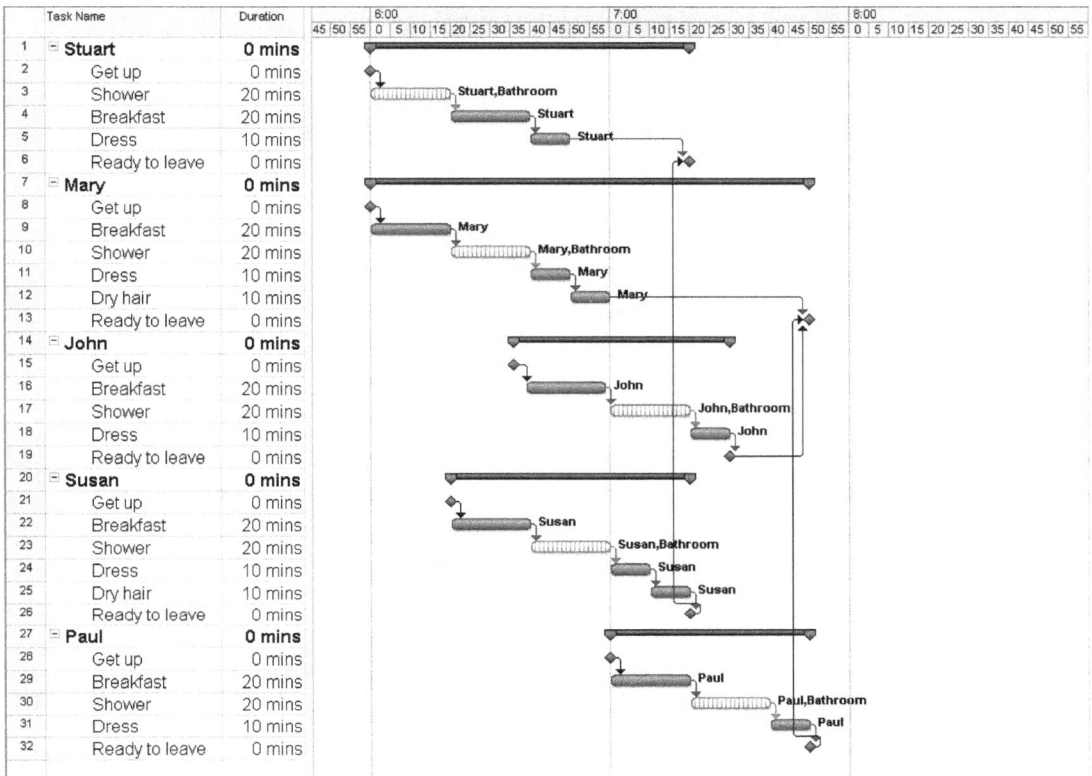

Figure 27 – Levelling: stage three

This picture shows the final version of the plan and it is surprisingly close to what happens in real life. Everyone is happy, even John, who quite likes some quiet time after he's ready to steel himself for the day ahead. The adults have a bit of time to kill but there's always plenty for us to do.

Applying the technique to a real project can throw up the same sorts of issues. Perhaps Paul is a temporary member of staff employed just for this project. This version of the plan uses him in the most efficient way – you only employ him for the minimum length of time. The down side to this is that all of his tasks are critical. There is absolutely no margin for error. An earlier version has more slack but is only workable if you can employ Paul as and when. It could work if he were a self-employed consultant, for example. And with slack in the project, there is a safety net if things start to go wrong.

--- ☆ ☆ ☆ ---

The point of the exercise is to show that with a limited resource (the bathroom) the initial stab at the plan can be quite different from the final version.[10]

If the plan is now unacceptably long, what can we do? Our other option is to increase the resource in some way. In the bathroom example one possible option would be to install a second bathroom as that would clearly have a big impact on the programme. Out of interest I added a second bathroom to the resource list, re-levelled and came up with the plan in

---

[10] And no, I didn't plan the morning with a Gannt chart. Remember my comment about a celebratory meal being a project? We sat around the table and worked our plan out over tea one day. I thought it would make a fun example, and it was quite scary the way it turned out to be so accurate.

Figure 28. Note that there are now two people in a bathroom at any one time and that the length of the project has reduced by about 30 minutes. So it would certainly help, but there are financial and space considerations. Is it worth the expense and disruption in order to have a couple more minutes in bed every morning? In the case of this example we decided that we would go with the plan in Figure 27 and get up early!

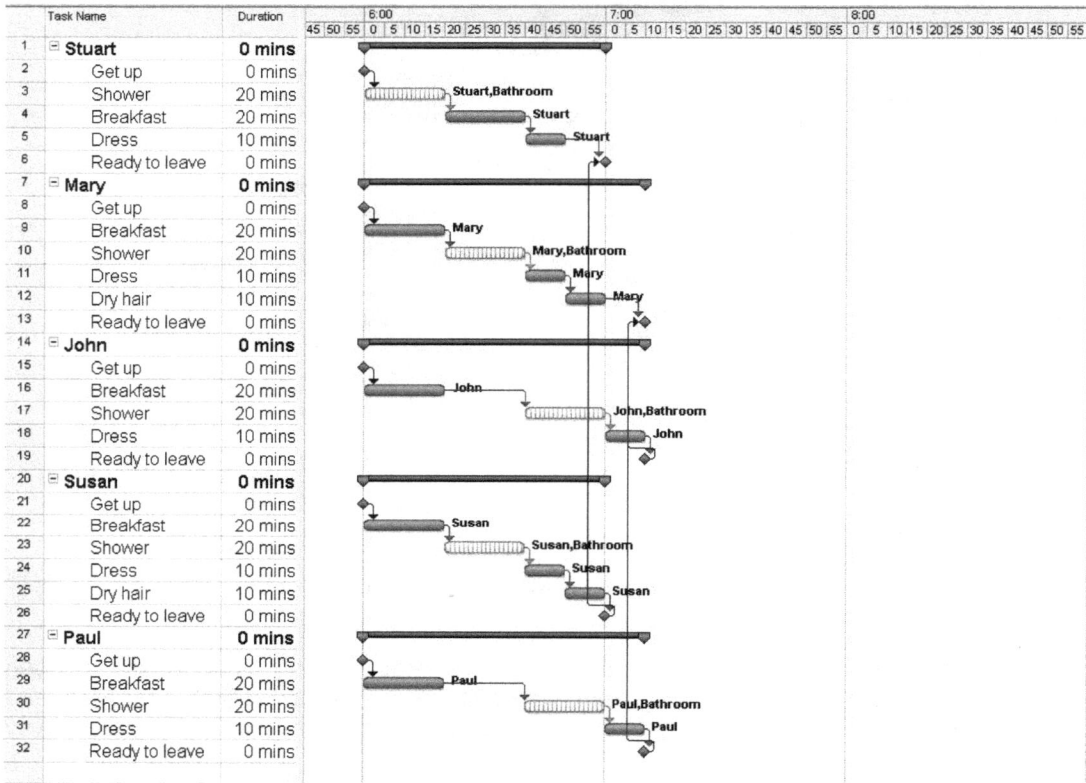

Figure 28 – Levelling: stage four; 2 bathrooms

In real life you will make similar sorts of decisions. Can we afford an extra resource in order to bring the project in earlier? Is time the critical factor, or can we happily let the project take as long as it takes? What are the financial implications of that decision?

Putting the draft schedule together

Going back to your project, by now you should have a schedule that shows sensible dependencies between tasks and also which resources are required for each task. You've levelled it so that it is a fair representation of reality – you have your first draft plan. Rejoice!

Schedule checklist

Before you go to the next stage run it through the following check list.

- The timescale predicted by the project plan is achievable

- All significant tasks are included

- The tasks are in the correct logical sequence

- The dependencies between the tasks are correct

- The level of detail is right

- The plan is visually effective

- The plan highlights priorities

- The critical path is visible

- The people involved have been part of the planning process

If your plan passes all these tests then you have a pretty good plan, certainly good enough to start with.

Budget planning

One major consideration is still missing. How much is all this going to cost? Let's look at putting the project budget together.

This is probably the one of the hardest bits of project management. Just how do you estimate for something which, by definition, is new? All you can do is base your estimates on similar projects that happened in the past, taking account of the mess they got into and resolving not to repeat it this time! Sorry, the cynic in me escaped for a moment.

Before getting to this stage, you should have a good idea of the duration of each task and the sort of person who will be carrying it out.

The person in your organisation who deals with the numbers will be able to give you estimates for staff costs and the on-costs you need to add in. On-costs take into account the fact that people cost more than their salary. Staff consume heat, light, and other resources, and they cost the organisation money in terms of pension contributions, etc. All these are real costs that the organisation has to cover for employing people and your project should reflect the real cost of its staff.

When you calculate costs for a project think about:

*   Equipment - what about the cost of computers, paper, photocopiers that the people use for the project?

*   Materials - if your project is to produce something tangible then the material cost should be clear. If it's intangible then there might still be material cost, e.g. a self-help group might have a newsletter (paper, staples, postage), coffee, room hire, etc.

If you have to buy hardware, get a number of quotes from people you trust. Add some contingency to allow for things you can't think of at the moment. For example, if you're buying a computer you'll certainly need software, but you'll also probably need cables and connectors, and you won't necessarily know what you need at the start. The contingency covers bits and pieces like this.

If your project is geographically spread, you are going to need travel and accommodation costs so don't forget to add those in. Remember to include travelling time to the project plan as a task.

And finally, add in some time for management. Project review meetings cost money and some of the attendees may be senior management and their time tends to be expensive. It all needs to be included somewhere in the project budget.

Full cost recovery

This is really important but outside the scope of this book. Suffice to say that if you are providing a service to a government agency, then it is wrong for you to subsidise that project out of voluntary funding. You need to work out the full cost to your organisation and include this as part of your project budgeting. The full cost obviously includes the project costs but also your infrastructure costs – for example providing office space for your project workers, a contribution towards the costs of their management, book-keeping time, etc. There are methods and models around for you to use.

Plan for quality

This sounds daft – of course you'll plan for quality. What I mean here is that you plan for the best you can possibly deliver then, if things start to go wrong or if you aren't given sufficient time or budget from day one, then you can cut back on some of the 'nice to haves' and still deliver something worthwhile (think back to the biro vs. Waterman pen example)

If you plan and cost for quality then you have some room to manoeuvre later on if the project looks as though it will go over budget or over time. If you plan for the minimum you can get away with and your budget is constrained, or something goes wrong in the project, you have no room to manoeuvre.

Optimistic estimating

When it comes to estimating time for a job, people are notoriously optimistic and will almost invariably underestimate the amount of time a particular task will take.

Here are a few guidelines

1. Only ever budget for about 80% of a full time person's time. So even if young Fred is assigned to your project full-time only expect him to work to 80% capacity. The rest of the time will be taken up with holidays, sickness, departmental meetings, etc.

2. In an ideal world you will know who's on your team and what their capabilities are. In real life this doesn't happen. However, you can still make reasonable estimates if you think of the type of person who will be working in your team. If you know, for example, that you'll be recruiting for the team, are you looking for experienced people who will know what they're doing? Or less experienced, and cheaper staff who will probably take longer and need more assistance?

3. Experience is the key. If you've done this sort of thing before, you'll make better estimates. If you haven't, the best bet is to find someone who has and pick their brains. If you haven't this luxury, then err on the cautious side.

4. You should not accept estimates blindly – you must evaluate them carefully. It is no good at all being optimistic with estimates. It is you who will get it in the neck if the project runs late – make sure you are happy with the time estimates. Realistic estimates that are correct, even if they aren't palatable to the management, are much, much better than hopelessly optimistic estimates that are wrong.

> In the software development industry there's a rule for estimating duration. It sounds far-fetched but I promise it's true and it works. It goes – if an engineer gives you an estimate, double the figure, and use the next largest unit of time. For example, young Fred tells you he can do the job in 2 days. For your project plan, allow 4 weeks. It sounds extreme but it comes from years of experience and takes into account all the activities that the engineer wouldn't think of, like documentation, testing, etc! It's obviously not the same in the voluntary sector but the principle is still valid.

Putting the budget together

The first thing to say is that when you put together a budget, it's important to include everything that will cost you on your project. Sounds a daft thing to say as it's blindingly obvious, but you'd be surprised how often a budget only covers half the story.

Let's start with the two basic types of cost: fixed and variable.

Fixed cost is something that you will have to incur no matter how long the project or how many people are on it. Variable cost depends on how long the project is, how many deliverables, how many people, etc.

It's best explained by an example.

Suppose your project is to produce posters for a marketing campaign. Part of the process is printing the posters. Most printers charge a set-up cost, then a cost per 1,000. The set-up cost is a fixed cost; you pay it whether you print 1,000 or 20,000 posters. The cost per 1,000 is clearly a variable cost. When you come to put the budget together, you need to take into account the difference between fixed and variable.

So how do you do it? The most straightforward way to put a budget together (note I didn't say easiest!) is to start with the plan. You've already checked that all the tasks are there. Are there any tasks that have fixed costs? Make a note of these. Now have you any variable costs? Finally, look at the human cost. In the voluntary sector this is likely to be the largest cost element. Look at each task and who you have assigned to it then allocate the appropriate cost.

Costing human resource.

The cost of a person on your project is not their salary. Each person your organisation employs costs a lot more than their salary. There's national insurance contributions, payments the company makes to their pension scheme, season ticket loan costs, and so on.

And there's the support staff they need, the person who does the books for the organisation, the secretarial help. In the commercial world there are 'direct' staff and 'indirect' staff. Direct staff earn money for the company: sales people, manufacturing people, etc. Indirect people are necessary costs to the company: accounts, cleaners, etc. The costs of indirect staff are spread over the direct staff to come up with a 'loaded labour rate'. It's this figure that the company uses to cost its operations.

In the voluntary sector we don't earn money in the same way but it could be useful to look at the project workers as direct staff and the support staff as indirect. In this way you can come up with a loaded labour rate for your project staff. This is the real cost to the organisation of employing the project staff. You may get objections from funders but you can't have a project person without the payroll/accounts/secretarial function to support him/her, so it is a legitimate cost that must be covered.

Infrastructure costs

How do you cost for these 'extras'?

A simple but effective way is to work out the costs of your organisation that don't get picked up directly by the project and allocate a proportion of those costs to your project. For example, if your rent is £1,200 per year and you have 12 people working full time in your office it's not unreasonable to allocate £100 per year per person. If one person is full time on project X then project X should pick up the £100. Similarly for heat, light, maintenance, etc.

If one of your 12 people is devoted to admin work and s/he spends half his/her time on project X then it's not unreasonable to charge project X with half his/her time – and half his/her on-costs.

Another way to do this is to collect all your organisation's overhead costs and apportion them per square foot (or metre) of your office space. You can figure out what proportion of the office is used by your project, and apply that to the overhead costs to get the charge for your project.

There are many ways, but the important thing is however you do it, it must be fair. You might have to justify your calculation in front of a potentially hostile audience at some stage; trustees, members, funders, etc. If you can show that you've acted fairly with regard to this project, you should be ok.

Once you've done all this you will have a cost per person. Depending on the length of your project and/or the size of the tasks, you may wish to calculate a weekly/daily/hourly rate for each of your people.

The extras that often get forgotten

The sorts of things that are often forgotten are travel costs, meeting costs, etc. If your project is scattered across the country there will be a considerable amount of travel expenses. Do you pay volunteers expenses? How about hiring meeting rooms? You've probably remembered room costs for tasks such as workshops, training courses, but what about the project review meetings?

And finally, don't forget yourself. You may not be shown on any tasks but you are a cost to the project. You will be spending a lot of your time managing the project and you cost your organisation money, which has to be budgeted.

Now you can go through the plan and figure out the human costs of your project.

When you do the grand adding up you will have your first stab at the budget. Keep it to yourself for now because you need to refine it.

Contingency

You now have a plan that seems to hang together. No-one is working 90 hours a week and none of your resource is double booked.

Sorry, but you haven't finished yet. No matter how detailed your planning, there is certainly something you will have overlooked. It can be something silly like you will be operating in Europe and forgot to add a continental mains adapter to the shopping list. It could be something major like the builders discovering something horrible when they take down a partition.

You need to put some contingency in your plan to try to cope with things like this. How much depends on so many things. If you've done this sort of project before you will have historical data to look at. You will (hopefully) have learned from your previous experience and will be able to judge fairly accurately how much contingency to put in.

Consider my old favourite: decorating a room. I estimate the area of wall I am going to paint, consult the tin to see what the manufacturer's reckon the coverage rate is, and work out how many tins I need; and then I buy extra. The first time I did this I bought quite a lot extra and had plenty left over, which sat in the shed for a few years until we cleared it out. As I did more decorating, my estimating got better and I got cuter. I would buy big tins and little tins, and the little tins would be my contingency. If I didn't need them at all, I could take them back for a refund.

This is exactly the same principle you will follow. As your experience in a particular type of project grows, you will need less contingency and your aim is to refund the organisation at the end of the project.

Adding contingency to the time a task will take will affect the budget. More time means more labour which means more cost. Also just throwing in 10% on top of a budget figure has the potential to affect the resource allocation. If a task costs more it's likely that it's because it requires more work, which means your labour isn't available for the next task.

It's relatively easy to put contingency in the budget. Just add a percentage of the costs, but don't forget that adding contingency time also has an effect on the budget. If you put in a couple of weeks extra time, then what about the staff who will be working that extra time? You need to add in a couple of weeks of their costs as well, and of course, a couple of weeks extra of your costs, too.

Important note about contingency.

It's not there for you to use. It's a safety net. It tells your organisation that this is the worst case you can think of and that if everything goes well you should be able to return the contingency budget to the organisation at the end of the project. If things go wrong then the organisation has already budgeted that money and so won't be hit by a horrible surprise. It should be your personal (and possibly secret) goal to not use it.

Your first draft

If you make it through to here then you've got a project plan that seems to hang together. You're pretty sure it's complete and it reflects what you have to do, when you have to do it and what you have to do it with. If you complete all the tasks on the plan you will complete the project.

You have your draft budget. Go back and look again at your plan. Are you sure it's complete? Are you happy with your contingency planning? Is there anything there that will have to be added to the budget? Does it make sense? Have you taken inflation into consideration? What about exchange rates and bank rates?

If you're happy with all this publish your plan! Make sure your whole team is aware of it. Put an issue number on it (because it will surely change throughout the life of the project) and start managing.

Software – a very brief mention

Budgeting

For a small project the budgeting process is not too difficult. It may be tedious but it's not difficult. As the number of tasks grows and the number of staff members grows, it gets more and more complex and it gets easier to make a mistake. This is where software can help you. Spreadsheets are a great way to make lots of calculations and they're easy to change. Project management software has budgeting built in. You can allocate costs to resources and the software will work out the costs to the tasks, etc. It can be worth using software just for this.

Scheduling

There is project management software by the ton out there. Scheduling is what it's best at. Software can certainly make your life easier but it has a downside. The algorithms inside the software are not under your control and they can sometimes produce some "interesting" effects. I have personally spent a couple of days fighting Microsoft Project when it produced an answer that was quite clearly bonkers but neither I nor my assistant could figure out why. In the end we discovered a tiny, tiny configuration glitch, and that cured the problem. But my point is it took days to find it. This sort of thing could easily happen to you and it could take you away from your main purpose.

Having said that, software does Critical Path Analysis in a flash – and usually gets it right. It's entirely possible to do critical path analysis by hand but it's tedious and it's only really practical for a small project. Anything more than a few tasks and you'll probably not bother checking it very often, and then the critical path will change and you won't notice. This will result in a SURPRISE – which we don't want.

One final phrase on software, a phrase coined when computers filled a room, but still 100% valid today:

> # GIGO : garbage in – garbage out

You need to understand what you're doing before you use a machine so you can spot when you're getting garbage. And that's why we spent time doing the examples earlier in the chapter by hand.

There's a whole chapter on software later, starting on page 100.

STAGE: TEAM BUILDING - Project teams

Team building is a really important part of your job. To do the subject real justice would triple the length of this book and there are many, many good books out there. I'm not re-inventing the wheel but there are just a few points I'd like to make.

A project manager makes things happen – he/she rarely does everything himself/herself. A project manager gets the team to do it and so needs some special skills. If you don't have a team yet it's still worth reading this bit as you will probably need to get people to do things for you. And if you have a team you must realise that although you carry the can for the project, you will rarely do all of the work and you need to know how to manage people who don't always work for you.

A good project manager

What makes a good project manager? Apart from being able to plan, schedule, problem solve, etc, a good project manager needs to have a number of people and personal skills. For example ...

- Leadership

    This is arguably the most important quality of all. It is *your* job to bring the project in on time and on budget and you need your team to deliver for you. If you are a good leader then your life as a project manager will be easier. Leading by example is a great way to motivate your team and to get the job done.

    Some people are lucky and just seem to be born leaders. Others have to work hard to do it. There are books, etc out there to help you. As they're always changing, I'm not including references here but there's information on the website[11].

- Relationship management

    Project team staff rarely work for the project manager so you need to develop and foster relationships with other managers across and outside the organisation, to ensure that your project is a priority and that the members of your team are not poached by others, or side-tracked onto other tasks.

- Influencing

    Often your team members will have conflicting priorities. You need to be good at persuading others that it's in their interest to place your project's needs at the top of their lists.

- Politics

    You need to assess the political environment in your organisation and understand the power structures. In order to keep your project alive you need to maintain visibility and manage the perceptions of interested parties. Give the impression of success – no-one likes to be associated with a failure and that includes the managers of your team.

- Communication

    You have to be good at communicating – a large part of a project manager's job is about communicating.

---

[11] www.3rdsectorskills.com

- Motivation

  There are times when it just all seems too much. All your team's paperwork seems to be in their 'too difficult' trays. This is when they need their project manager to swing by and get them moving again. If it's your job to motivate, how do you do it? The full answer is outside the scope of this book but one really good idea is to assign realistic and achievable tasks to people and make them responsible for delivering. Remember they may have to do other work at the same time as working on your project, and also that their ultimate loyalty is probably not to you but to their line manager. You need to be aware of this conflict of interest and work around it.

- Negotiation

  You need negotiation skills on two fronts; internally, with line managers for the resource you need and externally, with the customer when you need to balance time, scope and budget. You need to manage the customer's expectation so when the product is finally delivered he is not disappointed. And the most important thing to remember is 'think win-win'; there's no point putting something over on the other person because next time you want something, you know just what he/she is going to say to you.

- Facilitation of team working

  You may have a team from many disciplines. You can't treat finance people the same way as you treat family advice workers. You have to know how to get them to work together as a team.

  Each team member should have

  - a role in the overall plan
  - SMART objectives
  - authority to act on behalf of the project
  - a sense of commitment
  - understanding of expectations
  - responsibility to report to you on progress

Yet more things to be good at

- Shaping goals

  The goals you set your team members have to be SMART and applicable to them. You can't just regurgitate the project objectives and expect people to buy into them.   You need to make sure that your individual team members understand what you require from them, and you need to be sure that you cover everything when you do this exercise. Note that you may also have to take some of the objectives set by their line manager and adapt or re-word them to suit your project.

- Obtaining resources

  You may not have your own resources – other managers have resources. You need to get them! You need to bring all your sneaky talents to bear here to persuade, cajole or intimidate other managers into giving you the resources you need to deliver the project. Don't feel guilty – they would do the same to you, and probably have done.

- Building roles and structures

    For the length of the project your team takes on a life of its own, with roles and responsibilities outside the norm of the members' everyday lives. If these are real and meaningful, the members of your team will feel like team members and the project stands a better chance of success. It also gives the members of your team a better view of the whole picture when they understand who does what, and it helps you make sure that there are no cracks for things to fall down.

- Establishing good communication

    It's not enough to be good at communicating, you have to make sure it happens throughout your team, which is why it gets a second mention in this list. There's a whole section on communication later in the book (page 85).

- Seeing the whole picture

    You are in a unique position as project manager – you have overall responsibility and you are probably the only person who sees the whole project, who knows what all the issues, constraints, deliverables, etc are. You need to ensure you keep the whole project in mind at all times and that you don't get bogged down in unnecessary details.

- Problem solving

    Despite all your hard work in the planning stage, your project will run into problems and a good project manager needs to be good at solving them, spotting solutions and coming up with alternatives.

- Moving things forward

    Someone has to un-bung things when they're bunged up, and this someone is you! You have to be prepared to roll up your sleeves and get stuck in when things go awry. Apart from getting the project moving it's also good for morale for the team to see you getting your hands dirty (see leadership above).

Project team

A team is a collection of people, all with different strengths and weaknesses. When you're putting your team together you need to take into account the skills you need – surveyor, assessor, writer, etc. But as well as all these skills you need to consider the personal skills of your team. A man called Belbin did a lot of research on people at work and their roles and came up with a list of types of people, defined by their attributes. (There's a table on page 70 listing these attributes) Although we are all a mix of all sorts of attributes, Belbin stated that one of these categories dominated our approach to work. He then went on to suggest that a really first class team has all of these types within its membership.

If you go to the Belbin website,[12] you will find tests that you can do to find out what type you are, and it's worth doing at some stage. But you can get a good idea by looking at the table and observing your team. You can see from the table that the contributions made by each type complement each other.

Which one are you? If you know your natural type then you will have a good idea of what will come easily to you and what you need to work at. The same applies to your team. Ideally you will be allowed to choose from a large pool of staff and populate your team with one of each Belbin type. To quote one of my teenagers; "Yeah, right!". It doesn't happen in real life. But what you *can* do is look around your team and see what type each one most closely represents. If you have this information it will help you support them and it will

---

[12] www.belbin.com

enable you to see what gaps the team has. It's pretty unlikely that you'll have a full set on your team so someone (guess who?) needs to make sure the missing functions are carried out to ensure the team works well.

Dealing with senior management

We all have senior management. Sometimes they are the senior management of your organisation, sometimes they are the trustees and sometimes they can be external to your organisation. Whoever they are, they can help you or hinder you.

They can offer you support and encouragement, which is wonderful and a really good place to be. If you are in this situation you feel you can do what is right for the project and the organisation and you know you'll get senior management backing. Fantastic.

Or they can hinder you, in obvious or in subtle ways.

Hindering takes a few forms. There's out and out sabotage which is fairly easy to spot, although not always. They can 'help' (aaaargh!), which is usually worse. Micro-management is a horrible thing to suffer. This is where the boss gets amongst your people and tells them what to do, totally undermining you. The only way to get around this is to (a) quit (bit drastic) or (b) have it out with them. Something along the lines of "you pay me to manage this project, please let me do it". Only slightly better, but still very bad, is to allow your customer to dictate how you will manage your project. This is a difficult one, as sometimes your customer is your funder, but they have to understand that they are paying you to deliver a project. You, as the project manager, are the expert here. You need to be allowed to work in your own way to deliver.

This is not an easy area. Senior management have a major influence on how your career will progress so they're not to be upset. But they can also drive you insane. How to manage them is outside the scope of this book but be aware of the effect they can have on your project.

Belbin's team roles

Belbin Team-Role Type	Contributions	Allowable Weaknesses
PLANT	Creative, imaginative, unorthodox. Solves difficult problems.	Ignores incidentals. Too pre-occupied to communicate effectively.
CO-ORDINATOR	Mature, confident, a good chairperson. Clarifies goals, promotes decision-making, delegates well.	Can often be seen as manipulative. Offloads personal work.
MONITOR EVALUATOR	Sober, strategic and discerning. Sees all options. Judges accurately.	Lacks drive and ability to inspire others.
IMPLEMENTER	Disciplined, reliable, conservative and efficient. Turns ideas into practical actions.	Somewhat inflexible. Slow to respond to new possibilities.
COMPLETER FINISHER	Painstaking, conscientious, anxious. Searches out errors and omissions. Delivers on time.	Inclined to worry unduly. Reluctant to delegate.
RESOURCE INVESTIGATOR	Extrovert, enthusiastic, communicative. Explores opportunities. Develops contacts.	Over - optimistic. Loses interest once initial enthusiasm has passed.
SHAPER	Challenging, dynamic, thrives on pressure. The drive and courage to overcome obstacles.	Prone to provocation. Offends people's feelings.
TEAMWORKER	Co-operative, mild, perceptive and diplomatic. Listens, builds, averts friction.	Indecisive in crunch situations.
SPECIALIST	Single-minded, self-starting, dedicated. Provides knowledge and skills that are in rare supply.	Contributes only on a narrow front. Dwells on technicalities.

STAGE: CONTROL - Controlling your project

In this chapter we'll look at how to control a project once it's running. We'll look at monitoring, the right questions to ask, tracking progress and reporting.

Monitoring as control

Controlling a project is easy: it must be, because the following diagram shows how to do it with only 5 boxes and 5 arrows.

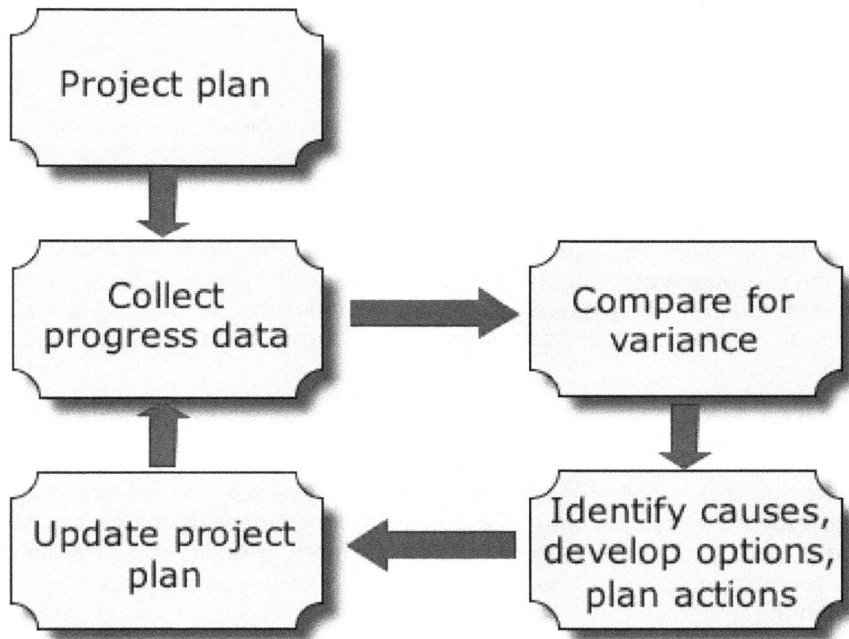

Figure 29 – Project Management in one diagram

All you have to do (!) is produce a plan, put it into action, then after a suitable interval see how you're doing against it. If there are differences between real life and your plan, figure out how you're going to fix them, update the plan, put it into action, and so on until you eventually run out of things to do, and the project is complete.

Easy, in theory. How do you go about it in practice?

Log book

Before you start get yourself a log book, something you can make notes in and record details of progress. My recommendation is a hardback notebook which should never leave your hand. This is where you record what you need to know about the project and you can also use it in evidence against people! For example, "…but you said last week" (leafing back through your book) "that this task would take only two more days…" etc.

What do you monitor against?

There are different levels of monitoring.

Milestones

At the top level, milestones are important events through the life of a project. There should not be too many or they lose their importance. But there should be enough so that if you meet all your milestones you generate confidence that you will complete the project on time.

You can use milestones to report on progress to senior management and your customer.

Examples

- Project specification signed off
- Equipment delivered and installed
- Project worker appointed
- First job placement achieved

There can be nothing woolly about a milestone. You achieve it or you don't. You can't partially hit a milestone. They are "*hit 'em or die trying*" issues. Think about hitting a milestone or getting hit with one if you fail! Senior management should give you a very hard time if you announce a slippage on a milestone.

Another use for a milestone is as a "gate". If you don't achieve the milestone you don't proceed to the next stage of the project. This is all very well in theory but if you get too hung up about gates you can find yourself ruining a project for the sake of the process. As with all these things, use the concept sensibly and it's great; follow it blindly and it's a recipe for disaster.

Lower level monitoring

At the lowest level you need to monitor everything. In practice, you will probably divide senior management milestones into smaller milestones which you monitor with your team on a regular basis. Remember that milestones are indicators that things are going well (or not). If one of your smaller milestones looks under threat then you have to dig deeper. As the project develops you will get an idea of which areas are strong and which areas need careful monitoring.

Questions to ask

People are, in general, nice and they want to please. If you think this sounds daft just think back to the last time Don or Margaret from Accounts asked you what you thought of their tie/outfit. You know it was dreadful but you didn't tell them, did you? (Did you??) Now replace Don/Margaret with a project manager. Do you want to admit to them that you're six days behind on a four day task? Of course not. You don't want to lie so you tell a sort of half truth, desperately trying to avoid upsetting them or dropping yourself in it. "Oh, I'm 50% complete", all the while crossing your fingers behind your back and promising you'll work extra hard to catch up.

So the moral of the story is: *don't ask "what percentage complete is your task?"* The person you're asking won't (usually) lie to you but they'll give you an answer they think you want to hear.

A better question is "How long will it take you to complete the task?" You are more likely to get a useful answer from this question. You still need to apply your 'fiddle factor' based on your knowledge of just how optimistic this particular person is but at least you're starting from a reasonable place.

It helps a lot if you can approach people with the attitude "What can I do to make it easy for you to deliver against the plan?"

Management by Walking Around (MBWA)

A popular management book in the 1980's coined the phrase 'Management By Walking Around' and the concept is as valid now as it ever was. If you sit at your desk you'll only know part of what's going on. If you wander around and talk to the project staff you will find out a lot more. One of the threads running through this book is the concept that project management is primarily about people. A good project manager spends time with their project staff, to help them with their tasks, and to get a feel for how things are going. With that feel, the project manager will be able to spot risks and plan to mitigate them. And that's what it's all about.

What to look for

Look for slippages against time and spending that differs from your budget and do something about them.

Time slippages

You're in the first month of a year long project and some of the tasks have slipped by a couple of days. Should you be worried?

The answer is a definite yes. You have just spent time putting together a project plan that represents the best estimates for all the individual tasks and it's going wrong already. Why is this? You need to find out the reason(s). It could be because the task depended on a machine that broke down. Is that machine used a lot in the project? Is it usually reliable? Should you look to the other tasks that rely on it? Or is it a one-off glitch? Can you recover the time? The answers to these questions are important as they may have implications for the rest of the project.

A more difficult situation is that the task just took longer than planned. You need to know why. Was the staff member unable to devote all their time to the task? Were they ill? Was the staff member sufficiently skilled to carry out the task in the allotted time? Was the time estimate clearly wrong? Can you recover the time?

It's really important to address these issues as they come up. Don't be swayed by the excuse "There's plenty of time. We don't have to deliver for x months." because if things go the way they seem to be going for the rest of the project you'll end up months late, and way over budget.

So the moral of the story is: *don't just accept slippages – ever.* Find out why they happened and take action.

Budget variances

At the end of each reporting period you should look at your budget. You should compare what you had planned to spend and what you actually spent. The difference is called the variance. Obviously overspend is a concern and you need to look at why you've overspent. Is it because the timing of the spend has changed but the overall forecast is still ok? Is it because you underestimated the cost of something? Is it because your staff are spending longer on tasks that you had estimated? There are lots of reasons for overspend and you need to know which apply to your project, and you need to know now so you can take action now.

Underspend is nice but should worry you too. Why aren't you spending what you thought you would need to spend? Is this a timing issue and you're suddenly going to get hit with a huge spend in a couple of weeks/months time? Has something not happened that should have happened? A lot of voluntary organisation underspend is failure to recruit and if you don't have the staff on schedule the impact on your project could be huge. Again, you need to know now so you can take action now.

Paperwork

Monitoring implies reports which means paperwork. This is where you can drown in paper – you don't need to.

- Keep reports brief
- Keep them simple
- Remember NO SURPRISES. This also applies to your management. If they are surprised, it's you they'll come looking for.

The ideal situation is where the paperwork you produce for your own benefit is enough to keep everyone else happy too.

One very important piece of paperwork is your log book. You can't remember everything in your head but you can remember everything if you write it down. And, as I said earlier, what you write down can be used as evidence!

Tracking progress

Project status reports

You are going to have to produce these and there are a few points to remember about status reports. First of all they are snapshots of the project in time. They're like an MOT – they tell you how the project is the day it was written and no more. In an ideal world you will have some sort of form for your project status reports. That will make them easier to write and easier to read.

How often should you produce them? Sometimes you have no choice and the decision is made for you by those on high. But if you have the decision then you need to think carefully. Too often and you'll spend more time writing the reports and less on managing the project. Too infrequent and they will be meaningless and leave you and the people who read them susceptible to surprises (and we all know what that means!)

Exception reporting is a good habit to get into and PRINCE2 promotes this approach. Try to educate your stakeholders to accept it. Exception reporting is all about not spending time writing about the stuff that's going according to plan and to budget. It's all about just reporting the things that are not. An exception report has the implicit message "it's all running to schedule/budget EXCEPT for…". Clearly an exception report will probably be mostly bad news or things to worry about, but you can run ahead of schedule and that's an exception too which needs to be reported.

You can usefully use a form for reporting, answering the following questions.

- Is project on schedule?
- Is project on budget?
- What are the major issues?
- What are the actions proposed to address the issues
- What are the major risks?
- What are the actions proposed to minimise risk?

If you are producing a report for a senior manager they shouldn't care about the detail. All they should want to know is "Is this project giving me/going to give me a problem – yes/no?" They need to know the basics so they can brief very senior managers, trustees, etc, and they need to feel comfortable that the project is under control. They also need to know the highlights so they can brag about your project to trustees, etc.

Share reports with your team

They need to know what's going on too. Team members will feel much more motivated if they know where their contribution fits in.

SOFT report

This is a reporting tool I have seen used to good effect particularly where there are a number of projects in progress. A single sheet of paper is used to highlight the Successes, Opportunities, Failures and Threats. Keeping it to a single page is a good way to concentrate the minds of those involved.

Here is an example of a SOFT report.

SUCCESSES	OPPORTUNITIES
New PC donated. Purchase price saved Risk 2 Local cable company confirm broadband available in this area. Risk downgraded to low from high, and reworded to "broadband installation may be late"	Spouse of trustee is web designer. May be able to save on design fee, depending on availability.
FAILURES	**THREATS**
Risk 105 Newsletter feature not available in this release of web design software. Upgrade to web software not available until August. Newsletter rescheduled for release 2 of website	Risk 74 Delay to purchase of domain name – issue with accounts re five year life of licence Risk 141 – new Will not know if trustee spouse can design website for another two weeks – dangerously close to deadline for engaging designer.

Figure 30 – SOFT report

This report is particularly useful if you have a number of projects on which to report. You can give your management a concise summary of the state of each project on a single sheet of paper or single slide. It gives you an opportunity to say how good things are (Successes), how rotten they are (Failures), what potential horrors the management need to know about and what you're proposing to do about them (Threats) and finally the wonderful Opportunities this project is presenting to the organisation.

Note that in this example the opportunities and threats both mention the spouse of a web designer that might be able to help us. This highlights a major issue for voluntary organisations. We all want something for nothing so it's really tempting to ask the spouse to do the work. But if that spouse found a paying job at the wrong time (for us, not the spouse) then s/he might understandably put our work off and that could cause havoc with our project schedule. In situations like this, when we are offered pro bono work, we have to weigh up the benefits and threats. Sometimes we have to refuse an offer for help, swallow hard and pay someone to do it instead because of the possible impact on the project.

Tracking progress

It's important to know how you are doing against the project plan, and Gannt charts (and to a lesser extent PERT charts) are useful for tracking progress. They give a good visual indicator of progress of the project. You should share them widely with the team and make sure all the team know how to interpret them. Most people have seen Gannt charts but some of the information they give is quite subtle. It may seem obvious to you but don't assume that all your team and all your stakeholders understand it.

Here is an example of a project plan. I've used Microsoft Project to generate these pictures because it's easy and they look nice. But this sort of reporting is just as good when the Gannt charts are hand-drawn.

Task Name	Duration	21 Feb '11	28 Feb '11	07 Mar '11
		S M T W T F S	S M T W T F S	S M T W T F S S
Collect material	5 days			
Prepare first draft	2 days			
Editorial meeting	1 day			
Prepare final draft	2 days			
Go/Nogo meeting	1 day			
Publication to printers	0 days			07/03

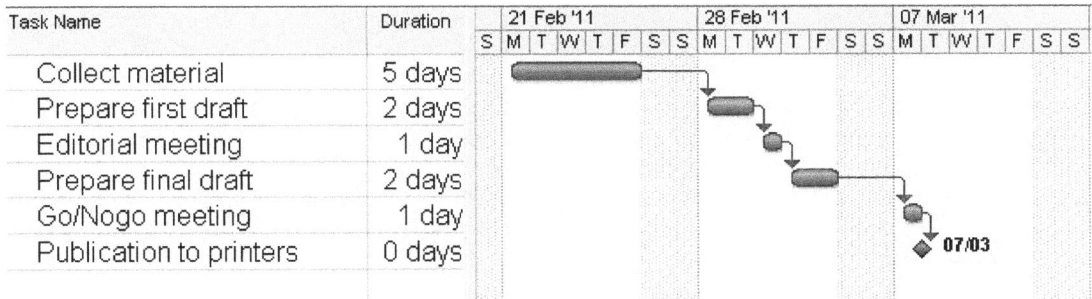

Figure 31 – Gannt chart as monitoring tool (1)

If you want to show progress all you need do is to mark the bars as the tasks are completed. You can use marks to show progress towards completion or if your chart is hand-drawn, highlight the completed tasks in a different colour.

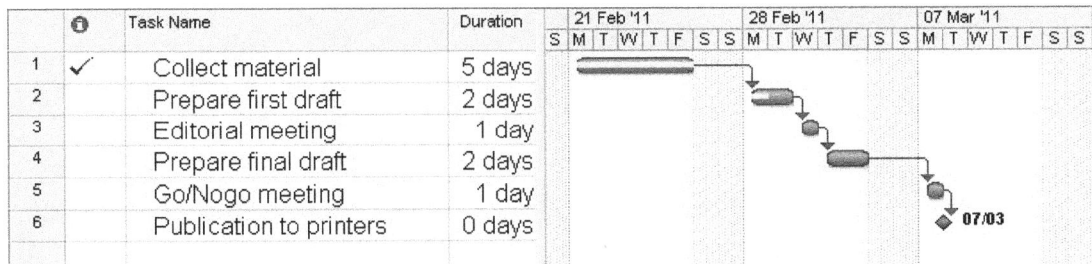

		Task Name	Duration	21 Feb '11	28 Feb '11	07 Mar '11
				S M T W T F S	S M T W T F S	S M T W T F S S
1	✓	Collect material	5 days			
2		Prepare first draft	2 days			
3		Editorial meeting	1 day			
4		Prepare final draft	2 days			
5		Go/Nogo meeting	1 day			
6		Publication to printers	0 days			07/03

Figure 32 – Gannt chart as monitoring tool (2)

The second chart shows that the material is all collected and the preparation of the first draft is well under way, possibly even half way done. If today is the 28th February then you could be excused for feeling quite good about life. Not so if today's the 2nd March – you're late!

Is the business case still valid?

You started this project off in order to satisfy a need: the business case for the project was carefully considered and it was agreed that it was valid at that time.

It's a really good idea to check from time to time that the business case is still valid. Have external or perhaps internal factors conspired against you and rendered the business case invalid? If so, is there any point committing your organisation's resources to continuing the project, or should you shut it down and go on to something else?

Project meetings

Project meetings are important. You just can't kick off a project and hope for the best. However much you try to resist you will have to have meetings during your project. As an absolute minimum you will need meetings to review the progress of the project, and to discuss issues and risks. Good meetings help the flow of information and help with sharing ideas and concerns. They can communicate the status of the project and shed light on what's coming up.

How many meetings you have and who attends them is dependent on the size/complexity/risks of your project. The trick is to get the right balance. Project meetings need to be

- Frequent enough to prevent surprises;
- Not so frequent as to take time away from achieving the work.

They don't always have to be face to face. People have slaved all their lives to bring new technology to you – use it!

- Teleconferences
- Video conferences
- Net meetings
- Combination of the above

Virtual meetings

Tip – try not to use virtual meetings until/unless the team know each other. If possible, get everyone together physically at an early stage so people can get to know one another. This makes teleconferencing much more effective. It's so much easier and more productive if the participants know each other.

Using this technology obviously saves travelling expenses and the time it takes participants to get to the meeting.

A good system is to have a small number of really detailed review meetings where you go through the plan to ensure that everyone knows how it is put together, what the risks are, etc. Then for the more regular meetings and reports you can just say "on schedule" and that will do. The people at the meeting or reading the report have been through it in detail; they don't need to be reminded every week. Just let them know you're on target and make sure you highlight any problems you can see coming up so that they can be prepared.

If you're not on target tell people what you're doing about it.

Some people will want to know more. Make it easy for them to find the information they want, preferably without involving you in additional work.

Successful meetings

There are people who make a good living training others how to run a successful meeting. The most important point is to plan it so that the result of the meeting is to add value to the project, not just waste everyone's time. Here are some of the key points are.

All participants begin the meeting:

- Prepared

  If participants show up to a meeting and then unseal the envelope in which you sent them the papers, they should be ceremonially flogged! There is no point turning up to a meeting without having prepared for it beforehand. It wastes everyone's time. The best participants have read the papers beforehand and have come prepared with questions or comments.

- Knowing why they're there

  How many times have you turned up to a meeting and wondered why you were invited? Don't do it to other people. People at a meeting should have a function, and a contribution to make, otherwise they are wasting their time and your organisation's money.

- Knowing what they are going to discuss

  This is back to preparation. If participants are prepared they will be more likely to make a useful contribution and might even push the project forward. They will know what they need to ask and have answers ready for others.

All participants leave the meeting knowing:

- What has to be done

  If a meeting produces no actions then why did you hold it? It's important to make sure that there is no doubt about what has to be done as a result. Think back to clarity of objectives – it's the same sort of thing.

- When it has to be done by – very important
- Who is going to do it

  You don't want any "I thought Fred was going to do that..." on your team. You need things to happen so make sure the participants know what they have to do.

Other good meeting practice

- Have an agenda published beforehand & don't have bald headings

  How much more useful to have an agenda item "Discussion of possible financial overrun and ways to resolve it" than an item labelled "Finance". A meaningful agenda item lets people prepare and you might get something useful out of the meeting rather than letting them come to the meeting 'cold'.

- Give plenty of notice

  Your team are all busy people so give them time to arrange their diaries if necessary.

- Start on time

  It's really rude and thoughtless to have people waiting around for a meeting to start. You owe it to them to start on time. If people are late don't go back to the beginning. They will have to catch up.

- Don't include people if they don't have to be there

  Don't waste people's time.

- Keep to the point

   There is nothing so irritating as people who wander off the point and start on about something completely unrelated to the subject. You're not there to talk about the football or the telly or even something else important in your organisation. You're there to review the project. Get on with it!

- Be prepared to create new meetings if required

   If there's a topic that only involves a couple of your team consider having a special meeting at another time, so as not to waste everyone else's time. If necessary you can arrange for a report on the special meeting to be circulated to the team members, or shared at the next full meeting so that everyone knows what is going on.

- Be prepared to cancel meetings if there's no point in having them

   If there is no point to having a meeting don't have one. Don't do it just because there's a slot in everyone's diary. I'm sure they will thank you for freeing a couple of hours in their week.

In summary, just be prepared.

Financial implications of meetings

Next time you're in a meeting that's going off the rails (not one of yours, naturally) count the number of people in the room.

If you assume that their average salary is £26,000 (carefully picked to make the maths easier!), then each member of staff costs your organisation £500 per week, or £100 per day. If you work an 8 hour day then each member of staff at the meeting costs £12.50 per hour and that's just salary. It doesn't include national insurance, pension contributions, office space, etc; all the 'on costs' which could easily double that figure.

If there are 8 people at the meeting then the meeting is costing your organisation a minimum of £100 every hour. How long does it take a tin-rattler to raise that sort of money?

Now get back to the point of the meeting...

Project review meeting agenda

You don't need a long and complicated agenda for a project review. The sorts of things you need to cover are:

- Actions from the last meeting

   What is the status of the actions agreed at the last meeting?

- Review of progress to date

   Are you on schedule and on budget? Any changes to the scope?

- Risks and issues

   What are the current risks and issues? Anything new? Anything been resolved?

- Work for the next week/month (or your selected period)

   What are you expecting to achieve in the next period of time?

- Review actions from this meeting

    What actions have come up during this meeting or have been carried over from the last? Who is assigned to each action? What is the timescale for each action?

- Date of next meeting

    Set a date, time and place for the next meeting

Alternative ways of holding meetings

You don't have to drag everybody into a room to hold a productive meeting. In many cases this is the most effective way because people can interact more easily if they're in the same room but face-to-face meetings can be expensive, particularly if attendees have had to travel any distance to get to it. There are other ways of doing it.

Audio conference

Audio conferences are a good way to hold review meetings at relatively low cost. They are not easy to cope with the first time you encounter them but, with a little practice and discipline, they can work very well. The users need to remember that they can't be seen at the other stations so visual gestures are out, and you need to identify who you are – not everybody will recognise your voice.

The simplest form of audio conference is to have a speaker phone each end of an ordinary call. You can then have two or three people at each end able to converse together. At the other end of the scale you can set up with your phone provider to link a number of different phones and in this way you can "conference in" people at many different locations. Conference calls work with mobiles so your staff don't even have to be at an office to take part.

This only works well if the equipment you're using is up to the job. If one telephone is a little ropey then the person using that piece of kit will be at a significant disadvantage.

One of the problems with audio conferencing is dealing with visual data – charts, graphs, even lists of issues.   Again, with a little thought this can be overcome. You might email all the relevant stuff beforehand but you need to be sure that it can be easily identified with only audio clues. For example, if you're in a face to face meeting you can point to part of a list, chart or diagram. If you're using audio conferencing you need to be able to describe where you're pointing, so use item numbers, colour, labels, etc.

Discipline is essential – it just doesn't work if more than one person speaks at a time. And make sure the room you're in is quiet. Use the mute button if you want to talk privately but make sure it works first!

There are lots of ways to get audio conferencing set up – all telecom providers worth their salt offer the service.

Video conferencing

It has been shown that 70% of all communication is non-verbal. Audio conferencing misses out on body language, so video conferencing is clearly better, but only if the kit you're using is good enough. You need to have decent quality video so you can actually see the person or people at the other end. Poor quality video linking is not worth the extra money over audio conferencing. Good quality video conferencing will enable you to have pretty close to a face-to-face meeting over a telephone line.

Net meetings

This is a recent offering from the computer world where you have a web cam at a PC at each location and you use the internet to have a one-to-one video conference. This has the big advantage of very low cost but the video quality is questionable. You can share files over the net so you can talk about pictures relatively easily.

Other methods

By the time you read this there will be more methods of holding meetings. The best way to keep up with the technology is to talk to a teenager! Alternatively look at the many productivity blogs on the internet, where you will always find the latest innovations. The 3rd Sector Skills website has some good links[13].

---

[13] www.3rdsectorskills.com

Maintaining the balance

Control is all about maintaining the balance between time, scope and budget. At some stage in your project you will probably have to do a bit of juggling.

We talked about the balancing act earlier in this book. If there is some major juggling to be done it can be a really good idea to involve your customer. There are times when he will, for his own reasons, be willing to sacrifice scope to maintain delivery on time.

Maintaining the balance and keeping all your stakeholders happy (or as near happy as possible) is a real skill. There are as many approaches to this as there are project managers. My own experience suggests that hiding things is not usually a good idea. Being "up-front" with your customer(s) may give you short-term pain but in the long run is more productive.

Changes

DO NOT – <u>EVER</u> – accept a change to the project requirements without first looking at the impact. Even the simplest change request can have major implications that are not immediately obvious. Is it worth the change if it delays the whole project?

<u>A minor change?</u>

Your project involves delivering material in ring binders, which are expensive. The original spec called for blue binders. You meet the person responsible for buying the binders and casually throw into the conversation "Oh, by the way, I was talking to John [your project's customer] the other day and they've changed the organisation's logo, so now we need to supply red binders. That's not a problem, I assume?" The buyer looks horrified. "But I've already bought the binders. Our office supplier had a special offer and I got them half price. They're sitting in the store cupboard already."

Your budget for binders is now blown unless you can persuade John to accept the original colour.

A silly example perhaps, but a couple of points come out of it. Firstly, you really should have known that the binders had been bought; and secondly, you should not have agreed to the change without checking first.

Now it's possible that your organisation can use the blue binders and you can recover the situation but it's one that should not have arisen in the first place.

Change control

Despite all your efforts some of the project issues raised are going to result in the need for a change. In my experience the chances of getting away without any changes is pretty much zero.

You must have a change control process in place. It need not be onerous but you must have one and you must enforce it. It must allow all those within the project who might be affected by the change to understand the implications, and advise you as project manager so you can decide what action to take. Although the project sponsor will have the ultimate authority on whether or not a change will be implemented, you must be the ultimate arbiter when it comes to approving changes because only you know the whole picture and can see knock-on effects that are invisible to others in your project team.

The change control process needs to be linked to the process for managing risks and issues since the resolution of many of these will result in changes to the project.

Some changes just have to happen, and you have to plan your way through them so that the impact on the project is minimised. Some changes are so major that you will need to go back to the project sponsor and/or the customer to discuss the implications with them.

Note, however, that not all changes are bad. Sometimes an idea for a change can be very beneficial to the product or to the project. However, you need to treat good changes with the same suspicion as bad changes until you're sure of their impact.

Some good changes can give you real problems particularly if they are suggested by members of your team. You may have to turn down a good change because the impact is too great and conveying this decision to the person who thought of it will require tact and diplomacy. Add these to the list of qualities a project manager needs.

Maintain a change request log

Keep a note of all change requests and what action was agreed. If the change was accepted keep a note of what the implications were and what the customer agreed to.

A change to your project may result in a change to the project acceptance criteria. Get the customer to agree to any of these changes so that, when the end comes, there is clarity about what the criteria are.

The change control mantra

> *NO!*
>
> *Not until I have analysed all the implications*

You need to be prepared to say NO. If this is not possible then you must try to renegotiate the scope of the project – more money, more time, less functionality, etc. This can be really difficult if your clients are likely to suffer because no voluntary organisation wants that. Unfortunately a change in project scope after the project has started is all too common (especially in this sector), and it's a very difficult thing to deal with.

It may be possible to implement the change as a post project update. And it may even be possible to extract some benefit to the organisation.

STAGE: COMMUNICATIONS - Project communications

One of the biggest jobs of a project manager is to make sure that everyone associated with the project knows what's going on, what they are supposed to be doing and when. And you need to be able to collect information in a timely manner from all those on the team. So communications is a big deal in project management.

Managing communications during the project

It's important to maintain communications with *all* stakeholders throughout the project. Remember that (in general) they want the project to succeed and they can help or hinder depending on how connected they feel to the project. If you keep people informed you can manage any conflicts that occur through the project life. You will ensure (as much as you can) that stakeholders remain positive towards the project.

Don't leave the project team out. Many project managers make the mistake of assuming that the team know what they're doing and how the project is going, and concentrate their communications efforts with management and customers. This is not necessarily the case and, even if it is, you'd be amazed how isolated team members can become. Keep them as up to date as your customer. In this way you can engage the team and this will aid problem solving. Don't distract them from their work but make sure they are kept abreast of good news and bad. They can be a great source of ideas to help the project along. Involve them in any changes to the plan.

It is in your interests to keep the communication channels open so that your team will keep you informed. You won't get all you need to know in those dreaded meetings.

Types of communication

In this section I'm considering primarily keeping people informed rather than collecting information. The type of communication method you use has to be appropriate to the project (size, complexity, etc). There seems to be little point being all formal and putting together amazing newsletters if there's only 3 people on the distribution list and they all work in the same building. But there's a good case for a newsletter if you have stakeholders scattered across the country. Under these circumstances you will need to think carefully how you will keep all your team up to date.

There are many ways to keep your stakeholders informed, and here are a selection

- Project review reports
- Bulletin boards (real or virtual)
- Presentations, meetings
- Newsletters
- Web based system
- Blog
- Podcast
- Social media (Facebook, Twitter, etc.)
- Wiki
- SharePoint/SocialText
- Other software products[14]

---

[14] The market is changing all the time, and there are always new ways of communicating with a team.

They all have their pros and cons. You need to consider the most effective way of maintaining communications with all of your project stakeholders. For example, I know of a project some years ago in the countryside when access to the internet was very limited. The few people who had computers were linked by dial-up lines. So there was very little point in going for a web based communication system. In fact, this project used Parish notice boards – very old fashioned, perhaps, but it worked.

Even if your project is based in a big city with lots of broadband access, don't assume that all your stakeholders have computers. If your project involves volunteers, is it fair to put all the documents on line and expect the recipients to print them out at home?

Your clients may also influence your communications strategy. People like my dear old Mum (aged about 80) doesn't understand computers or the internet. If I were running a project with people like her as clients, I would be wise to consider non-electronic communications – I might very well consider that the best means might be good old Postman Pat.

Web based systems

Social media

If you want to, or can, use a web-based system, then a blog is a good way to start. Most people think of blogs as a way to raise a charity's profile, raise funds, etc. They're normally targeted at Joe Public.

But you can also have a private blog that only you and your team can access. You can use posts to keep your people up-to-date. They can comment on the posts so there can be two-way communication. You can also give your team access to fixed information. You can link to project plans, documents, etc, anything that can be stored on a hard disc.

You could also use Twitter to keep your team up to date. The advantage of Twitter is that your team don't need to do anything. The information will pop up on their computer and alert them to the new information. You can use Twitter to tell your team of a new post on your blog.

This subject is vast and outside the scope of this book. If you want to know more, there are resources on the website[15]. It's the only way to keep up-to-date in this fast-changing area.

Cloud computing

This is an amazing way to share information. Again it's a huge area, but in essence it's putting your project's data on a server that's accessed via the internet. It means that, provided you have a web connection, you can access the information from anywhere and at any time. You can also keep diaries online, so your team can see where you are and when.

It's pointless to try to put this information in a paper book; it will be out of date by the time I finish typing this sentence. If you're interested in using this sort of technology in your project there are links and resources on the website[15].

Podcasts

If your clients have visual impairment, then you could prepare a podcast to let people know what's going on with your project. A podcast is essentially a mini-broadcast that you can prepare using your computer. At its simplest it's an audio file that you record and put on the web as an mp3 file. This means that you can play it on portable mp3 players (like the iPod and others), your mobile phone, and even your desktop or laptop computer.

---

[15] www.3rdsectorskills.com

You can link your podcast from a blog and/or Twitter.

Communication plan

> *Communication, to be effective,*
> *cannot be a haphazard process*
>
> *John Adair*[16]

Just like other facets of project management you need to plan your communication strategy. You need to know what the various stakeholders want/need to know in order that you can plan/manage how they will be kept informed. Because clarity is so important it is worth spending some time working on this at the outset of the project.

The detail of the communication plan will depend on lots of factors, for example

- Stakeholders – who are they and where are they located?
- Does your team have email or do you need another method?
- How long is the project timescale?
- How complex is the project?
- How big is your team?

Effective communication

So much for the means of communication. What about the content? It's really important to put yourself in the place of the person receiving the communication and structure all your content so that it will be understood. It seems obvious but they don't know what you know. If you try to see life from their point of view it is very likely that you will be able to communicate much better with them.

Remember the communication buzzwords:

- Clarity
- Brevity
- Empathy

Use simple language. Don't pontificate, obfuscate, discombobulate or perambulate around the subject matter. Remember one of Stuart's golden rules – KISS. It applies here, too.

There are plenty of stories about executives who only read reports if they are less than one side of paper. Bear that in mind when you communicate with busy people. Get to the point. If there's any need for follow up they'll be in touch, and you can drown them with all the backup material you like. But for now, make it snappy.

And again, empathise with your listener/reader and you'll be a successful communicator.

---

[16] John Adair's books are worth reading. He's one management guru who really makes sense.

STAGE: REVIEW - Reviewing your project

The project is under way. Now all you have to do is to sit back and watch your plan unfold...!

One thing I can guarantee is that if you just sit back and watch, your plan will disintegrate. To prevent this horror, you need to keep on top of your project and constantly review progress.

Reviewing the plan

Keep a close eye on the plan. Constantly monitor it against reality. Ask the people who are doing the work how they're getting on but don't take people's word for how far advanced they are. Probe, ask awkward questions and assess for yourself the progress. Compare progress against the plan and keep it up to date. Keep checking which is the critical path. It may change through the project.

Don't rely on people telling you what's going on. The best project managers I've seen are those who are 'out there' with the people doing the work (MBWA[17]), seeing for themselves what's happening. They are the ones who become aware of problems in advance and have that little extra time to plan their way around them. The worst thing you can do is just sit around and wait for information to get to you. Be proactive.

Reviewing the risk log and identifying problems

Projects are high risk activities so keep reviewing the risks. They are likely to change through the life of the project so don't just look at the risks already in the log. Have a periodic risk review to see if any new risks have appeared or if any have faded from the scene. It can be useful to cast your eye over the risk register at each project review meeting.

Keep the risk log up to date. It will help your peace of mind, help you convince yourself that you've thought of all the risks and you've planned how to avoid them or mitigate their effects.

Reviewing the budget

When you review the budget you need to know the answers to a few basic questions. Is your spending on schedule or are you ahead/behind budget? What are the reasons for any differences? Recognising that performance to date is no indicator of performance in the future, what are you forecasting for the end of the project, financially? Will you achieve the whole project on budget? If not, why not?

Collecting the information

How do you find the numbers? Essentially they split into two; those to do with your internal human resource, and everything else.

Capturing data on things you buy is relatively easy. You can track invoices for things you buy, add up the numbers and there's your answer.

Contracted labour is straightforward as long as they don't work on your site, because then all the costs are covered by an invoice. If you employ a contractor and s/he is based at your offices you should cost in the on-costs that you would apply to an ordinary employee. If

---

[17] Management By Walking Around – see page 74

you've gone through this exercise earlier, you should still have data on office and service costs per employee, and you can use this information for your financial reporting.

Your own employees are perhaps the hardest expense to track. HR departments are generally not keen on divulging individual's pay rates, so you may have to take an average and add on the on-costs to come up with a good approximation. You may get lucky and not have to worry about employee costs.

Whatever you do and however you do it, you can generally only come up with a 'pretty good idea' of your project costs unless you have a sophisticated cost collection system. In my experience a 'pretty good idea' is usually good enough, provided you are rigorous and thorough in your approach.

Presenting the budget information

How can you answer all these questions? I suggest you use a report like the one in Table 1. It shows you the details of your spending to date and then your forecast of spending to the end of the project. The first bit is easy – just collect the numbers from your accounts system. The forecasting is more interesting. You have to apply your experience of the project so far and look into the future. Most forecasting is based on the budget you originally had from here to the end of the project, plus some adjustments. Perhaps you know a payment that was due this month will not come until next month – you need to put this number in the forecast. If you find you've under or over budgeted something you need to put the adjusted figure in the forecast.

If I were your boss, it's these numbers that I would question most so be prepared to justify your assumptions.

People who work with numbers tend not to use minus signs in tables of numbers because they're hard to see. So they use brackets to indicate a negative number. In the report to follow, I've adopted the convention that BRACKETS ARE BAD. The variance calculation is set so that if the variance is negative, then it's bad news. So the income line 1 is lower than budgeted, hence the (500). The expenditure for line 4 is higher than expected so we have another (500). In my view taking this approach makes life so much easier. The spreadsheet is a little trickier to set up but the result is worth it. Now you can just scan the report and all the things you have to worry about are in brackets.

	So far			Project end		
Income	Budget	Actual	Variance	Budget	Forecast	Variance
Line 1	6,000	5,500	(500)	12,000	12,500	500
Line 2	200	350	150	400	750	350
Line 3	400	400	0	800	800	0
Total	6,600	6,250	(350)	13,200	14,050	850
Expenditure						
Line 4	4,000	4,500	(500)	8,000	9,000	(1,000)
Line 5	300	300	0	600	550	50
Line 6	500	450	50	1,000	800	200
Total	4,800	5,250	(450)	9,600	10,350	(750)
Surplus (Inc-Exp)	1,800	1,000	(800)	3,600	3,700	100

Table 1 – Project finance report

The 'so far' set of columns shows the situation as it is today. It is fact. The 'project end' set takes the budget from now until the end of the project and then takes what we think we will really spend/receive based on what's happened up until now; it's our forecast to the end of the project. And the last column tells us the difference between the budget and our new forecast.

This report gives you what you need to know about the project finances.

What does this report tell us?

It says that so far we are £800 behind on our budget; that is the project bank balance is £800 overdrawn right now. But we are forecasting that it will all come good in the end and the project will make a small surplus on budget.

If you're a big organisation with a budget in £millions, then £800 is probably not a major issue, because the project is forecast to come out roughly on budget. You can carry the project's overdraft without much pain.

However, if you're a small organisation, can you carry £800 for this project? Today, the fact that the forecast is pretty good is irrelevant. Today, you need to find £800 from somewhere to keep the organisation going. Today, you have bills to pay. Remember, cashflow is king.

Looking in more detail it would seem that lines 1 and 4 are the problems.

Line 1 is well under budget - £500 less income than expected. But scanning to the right shows that it comes good by the end of the project – possibly the glitch at the moment is a timing issue – a supplier late paying an invoice perhaps? Needs to be checked out to make sure that our assumptions for the forecast are valid.

Line 2 seems ok – a little bit ahead of budget. But £150 variance on a budget of only £200 is a huge percentage. We should know why that is the case.

Line 3 is on budget so not much to wonder about here.

Line 4 is the real worry. We're spending too much and we're going to continue spending too much. Is there really no scope for clawing back that £1000? Possibly there's a good reason for this. If we can't recover the overspend then this line is a definite candidate for the project evaluation meeting. We need to know what went wrong so we can try to make sure it doesn't happen in the next project.

Line 5 seems ok, and line 6 too, although it is forecast to come in 20% below budget – another candidate for the evaluation meeting.

Whether you are presenting or receiving this report you need to have an explanation for every variance. If there are lots of lines then you might concentrate on the biggest numbers but don't neglect the little ones – they can soon mount up and hurt you!

Reviewing the need for the project

Not only do you need to review the plan and the finances, it's also a very good idea to review the achievements of the project against the original idea – is the project still going to deliver the benefits it set out to deliver? Is the project still worth doing? Has the external climate changed and made the project's viability doubtful? Has the project exceeded expectations and now will it deliver more than expected?

Look at the business plan for the project. Is it still valid? If not, what impact does this have on the project? Should you revise any of the objectives? Should you change the scope of the project? At the extreme should you close the project prematurely?

The one thing you should never do is continue with a project just because you started it. Any project MUST deliver benefit to your organisation.

Problems

There will be problems and you need to keep on top of them. Some problems can be dealt with instantly. But others need to be passed to someone else, or thought about, or parked until the appropriate time. It's really important that these do not get lost. There's a simple system to help you prevent this.

Issue reports

Regard EVERY problem as a "project issue". Encourage every project member to raise an "Issue Report" whenever s/he is unsure about something or notices a problem. This could be serious or trivial but it's important that all uncertainty is sorted out.

Issues need to be looked at. Don't disregard any problem even if it seems minor. It is entirely possible that a minor problem left alone will grow into a major project issue.

For each issue you need to take action. Will you deal with it immediately because it's a showstopper and just has to be fixed? Does it need further investigation before you can make a decision on it? Is it a 'nice to have' that can wait to see if there's time or resource to deal with it? Whatever the issue you can't ignore it; you have to do something and it's important that you record what you do. And, although it may seem obvious, you need to consider the impact on the rest of the project of diverting some resource to deal with this issue – what's the knock-on effect of it?

If your project is small you can easily keep on top of issues with a simple log, similar to the risk log. If it's large you will probably need a more formal system. Whatever you do, you should write down all the issues as they arise. Assign a priority to them and deal with the urgent ones right away. You can collect the minor ones together and blitz them towards the end of the project.

An organisation I know used a paper-based system to record issues and the issue form was printed on yellow paper. This simple technique meant that the issue reports stood out in any pile of paper and made it very hard to lose track of them.

Dealing with problems

Problem solving in seven easy steps

If you have an issue you have a problem to solve, so let's have a brief digression on problem solving. In principle this is very easy – in practice, not quite the case!

1. Define the problem

Start with identifying the problem. This may sound blindingly obvious but you need to know what the real problem is before you can solve it - not what do you *think* it is but what it *really* is.

Example

A bank manager saw queues in his bank and noticed the customers were quite agitated. He decided the problem was a lack of cashiers and he re-jigged his staff rotas so there were more cashiers on duty at the peak times. He set a target to get queuing time to less than 5 minutes. A couple of weeks later he noticed that the queue time was shorter but the customers were still agitated. He then (!) thought of asking the customers why they were agitated and discovered that they were too hot. It was nice that the queue time was shorter but the main issue was the heat in the bank. All that effort to fix a problem that wasn't really there.

You need to ask dumb questions to find out what the root cause really is – a good one is "Why?" asked again and again. Keep on asking until there are no more to ask.

2. Identify possible causes

Now you know what the problem is, why is it happening? There may be a number of causes or just one. But that root cause may be hiding behind others so make sure you dig and dig until you find the thing that, if fixed, will solve your problem.

3. Re-define the problem to include the causes

"The customers in my bank are upset with us because the heating system is broken and the heat in the bank lobby is excessive."

This statement tells us that the problem is the heating and all we have to do is fix it.

4. Collect possible solutions

Brainstorming is a good way to collect all the possible solutions. Use the session to collect every idea, no matter how dumb it may sound, because the dumb ideas are often the simplest or they may spark off the best solution.

Fix the heating problem by

- opening the windows;
- installing fans;
- putting a refrigerator in the lobby and leaving the door open;
- fixing the thermostat.

Now in this case the solution is pretty obvious, but if it's going to take a while to get the heating fixed some of the other ideas might be useful. In real life you don't always get problems with easy solutions so it's worth considering this approach.

Example of lateral problem solving

A contractor had built a skyscraper in a large city. The new occupants were moving in and the contractor and new owners were dealing with little issues in finalising all the details of the contract. As the number of people in the building increased the office workers started complaining about the lifts being too slow.

Trying to make changes to the lifts would have been a pretty expensive modification. The people who had designed the building came in, timed the lifts and determined that they were operating as expected. However this did little to reduce the number of complaints and the designers set about trying to fix the problem. The looked at the cost of installing additional equipment to speed up the lifts. They also considered segregating some of the lifts as "express lifts" to only reach certain floors.

One bright individual stopped concentrating on the lifts and started paying attention to the people as they waited. After studying them for a while he made a suggestion - install mirrors outside the lifts on each floor. His suggestion was implemented and the complaints disappeared.

The mirrors did nothing to increase the speed of the lifts. They did give the riders something to do while they waited for the lift to arrive. They could look at themselves in the mirror. This seemingly minor change solved the real problem – people were bored.

---

5. Choose the best option

Now you have a range of options you can assess which is the best from all perspectives. In this example the really boring answer (fix the thermostat) is probably the one to go for. But this is not always the case.

6. Get agreement

If your solution involves anything more complicated than getting a thermostat fixed then it's a good idea to get your project stakeholders to agree on your decision, so that they will support you in doing what you have to do.

7. Implement

Get on with it!

There are lots and lots of books written about problem solving. Have a look at a few and pick the method that suits you and the situation.

Changes

There are times when you look at an issue and decide not to do anything about it. But sometimes, despite your best efforts, some problem or other will mean you need to make a change to the project. Before you do, ensure that you know the impact this change will have. If it's something the customer has introduced make sure that he knows the effect he is having on the project. Can you get extra time or money out of him?

If it's an internally generated change then you need to figure out a way of getting it done without changing the delivery date, costing more money or compromising the scope. Or you might have to come clean and admit to your customer there's a problem, work with him to resolve it and agree any changes to the project plan.

Make sure the change is recorded in the project brief. This document is the project rulebook and changes to the rules need to be recorded.

Make sure the whole team is aware of the change and any impact it has on them.

Finally, modify the plan and distribute it again to *all* stakeholders.

STAGE: HANDOVER & EXIT

This is a phase of the project which is often neglected. Certainly projects are handed over but many projects are ineffectively closed down, with consequent impact on the organisation. It's easy to see why proper close-down is not always done – once a project is near enough completed there are always more exciting things to do, like the next project. But a little time spent on closing down will deliver many benefits to your organisation and to you.

A project needs an end. You need to 'hand over the keys and walk away' from every project. For some, like opening a building of some sort (drop-in centre, headquarters, etc.) you can literally hand over the keys to the person in charge and that's the project milestone achieved. For others, like starting a new day service where the build up of service users may be slow, it's harder to identify the end point. Do you set it at the first user, the fifth, or when the service is 50% used?

And what about this handing over the keys idea? In the voluntary sector we often have many hats. If you are the project manager and the operations manager then what's the point of handing over keys to yourself? It's a good mind-game to play. Once the project is over you can free yourself from it and move into operations mode, which, as we discussed earlier, is different.

What is handed over and when?

For most projects there's a clear handover at the end of the project. But if your project is long, or large, or both, it can be useful to have mini-handovers throughout the life of the project, depending on its size and duration. Consider carefully what is handed over, to whom and at which stage of the project and what financial rewards you can extract from your customer at each stage – remember, cash flow is king. If you have significant financial outlay at any time you need to get your customer to pay for as much as possible at that time. You could use project milestones as points to factor in stage payments. We're in voluntary organisations – we can't afford to act as banker to statutory authorities or any other kind of funder.

Plan for a successful conclusion

This sounds daft, I know. Who would plan to fail? What I mean by this is that it's very important to FINISH the project and move on. Planning for a successful conclusion means making sure that everyone knows when you've finished. Make sure the conditions for final acceptance are agreed in advance so that everyone knows when you *have* finished, *including* the customer. Make sure the customer signs off the project with some sort of acceptance document. Then there can be no misunderstandings.

Dealing with unresolved issues

It's likely that there will be a few outstanding points at handover but if the project is largely complete then the normal thing to do is to close it down with a list of things to be fixed. In the commercial world the customer will usually withhold a percentage of the payment until these issues are satisfactorily resolved. You may be able to use this argument to get most of the payment for your project.

Make a list of all the outstanding issues, making sure that your description of each issue is absolutely clear and unambiguous, and also write down acceptance criteria for each issue – that is, what you have to do to resolve the issue to the customer's satisfaction. The idea of this is that if you comply with the acceptance criteria of all the outstanding issues there can be no doubt that you have fulfilled the project and you can claim any withheld funds and close the project down. A good example is a snagging list which is put together towards the end of any building project. It lists all the defects that the purchaser expects the builder to put right before the job is declared complete.

Delivering with style

Don't neglect the PR potential of a handover. You've just spent weeks or months of your life on this project. Don't just let it end with a phut! Make a noise about it. Make sure it has some sort of impact!

A handover is a great vehicle for:

- Positive publicity
- Fundraising potential
- Staff morale

Make sure you have included a handover celebration in the project plan with an associated budget. You want your organisation to reap the most benefit from the project conclusion.

Make sure your team know they've done a good job. A party doesn't have to be expensive and should have been in the budget from day one. It will do wonders for the organisation in all sorts of intangible ways. Besides all this, organising a party is fun and even project managers need to have fun sometimes. If you're uncomfortable using the organisation's funds for a party think of it as a grand PR exercise to raise awareness of the cause and use the fact that your staff and volunteers are there to help spread the word. It may be possible to get a sponsor for the event.

Just to put a damper on the festivities, don't assume everyone will feel good about a handover. Some project staff will move straight on to another task and won't feel the sense of satisfaction. Some of them will move on before the end, so try to involve everyone who contributed to the success no matter where they are now. And some will lose their jobs. Anyone employed on a fixed term contract may not be too delighted when the contract ends. At this stage you need to have your sensitivity set to maximum.

Acceptance certificate

I really like the idea of an acceptance certificate. You can easily knock something up on your favourite word processing software. Make it look impressive, with your logo all over it.

Why bother? Because you can add it to the project documentation and build up a portfolio of success. This will help your organisation when it goes for funding because you can demonstrate that you are good at what you do.

And on a personal note, you can demonstrate to future employers that you are good at what *you* do.

Closure

There are all sorts of good reasons why it's really important to close the project down properly. You don't want it limping along for ever, sapping the energy of the organisation and stopping you getting on with the next jobs.

Some things to look out for are:

- Make sure the staff stop working on the project.
- Make sure all the finance loose ends are cleared up. If you are sophisticated enough to have cost centres, shut them down. (This won't stop people working on the project; all they'll do is book to another project and make it over budget, but it

shows willing and besides, the other project manager will be keeping tabs on his/her budget and jump up and down on the offenders)

- Make sure the customer signs the final acceptance and pays the bill! This is also good for your customer as they can wave a piece of paper in front of their bosses and hopefully look good. Remember, if you make it easy for them to look good they'll be friendly towards you.

- Hold a final evaluation review so that any lessons learned can be passed on to the rest of the organisation. This is vital to the organisation.

- Make sure that, if the project is to be handed over to someone to keep going as part of the organisation's operations, all the relevant information is handed over and the responsibility for running the operation is clearly passed to the new team.

The closure meeting

A good agenda for the closure meeting is

1. Review outputs or outcomes

   Were they all as expected? Did the project deliver the planned benefits? If not, why not? Were the outcomes unrealistically set in the first place; if you had to do this project again would you set them differently? Were the outcomes reasonable but somehow you failed to achieve them all; why was that? What would you do next time to fix this?

   Any really good (or bad) points to consider? What was so good you want the whole organisation to change the way it works so it can take advantage of this good point? And conversely, what was so bad ...

2. Confirm arrangements for any follow-up work

   Agree list of outstanding issues (if any), and the acceptance criteria for resolving them.

   What about maintenance of equipment (if any)? Is there a contract in place? Is there a training requirement for staff?

3. Present completion report for formal sign-off

   This is the real end of the project when the customer signs it off as complete and may authorise the final payment.

4. Thank team, sponsor(s), stakeholders

   Don't forget this. You are the project manager but you couldn't have done it without all these other people.

Problems in closure

The product has been handed over but there are still some problems outstanding. If the team has been disbanded who will fix the problems? If the team is still together then they could continue to work on it, but where will the budget come from?

Project drift is all too easy. The project almost finishes but there is "one last little thing" that was probably not in the original spec. Remember the caution about changes earlier on? This is a classic area for customers slipping a change in and hoping no-one will notice. Extra tasks 'appear' and the project never really finishes. Resource leaks from the organisation to complete these little tasks. There is no budget so people get creative and other projects get charged for work that doesn't belong to them, and so their costs escalate.

The moral is: *close it and walk away from it, and make sure the rest of the organisation does the same.*

Evaluating the project

Only fools do not learn from history. Make sure you're not a fool.

It is very easy to skip this step. There is always something urgent that makes this step fade into the background. Don't let it happen to you. Both you and the organisation will benefit from some time spent evaluating the project.

Questions to ask

If you're evaluating a project you want to know both the good and bad points - the good, so you can do them again, and the bad, so you don't.

- What went well/badly and why? Although not a time for blame, this is a good time to admit your own mistakes. If something went well then how can you spread the good practice around the organisation? If something went badly then could it have been done differently, and presumably better?
- What should we do/never do again?
- Were the systems/tools helpful or not? Talk to your customers and suppliers. They may have some useful insights and suggestions on how to do better next time. Are there processes within your organisation that, if modified, would make running the next project more straightforward?
- Were all the expected benefits realised? Did the project deliver all it was supposed to? If not, why not? Were the objectives too ambitious? Did the external climate change during the life of the project to reduce its overall effectiveness?

It may be that the full benefits of your project will not be apparent until some time after the end of the project, so you may want to schedule a review a few weeks/months later.

Don't file and forget

Once the evaluation is complete don't just file the report. You need to make the organisation aware of your conclusions. If you have a system of regular meetings, perhaps you can take a slot at one of these or make a special presentation to the rest of the organisation so they can benefit from your experience. And once again, don't neglect your team. They can also benefit from the experience.

Write it up – the portfolio of success

It is well worthwhile spending some time writing up the project. You can use the finished report:

- as a case study to help promote your cause. For example, when some people were moved from an old residential home to a new development the process went superbly well, and the people were very happy with the end result. The charity involved asked a university professor to write a report on the project to show what could be done, why it's worth investing in such projects, and how the taxpayer got a really good deal out of the project. The study was then used to show the effectiveness of the solution, and the charity's expertise.
- as an example of your expertise when it comes to moving to a new job (it does no harm to keep a portfolio of success).
- to support your organisation's bids for future funding (it's a competitive market out there and you need to show that your organisation can do a good job and give value for money to funders).

Dismantling the team

Dismantling a team can be an emotional experience for the team members and the person doing the dismantling. It is not good to just let the team evaporate. It's best for all concerned to be seen to actually take it apart – it provides closure.

Remember that if you have had staff employed just for this project they may need references for their next job or support in reviewing their careers. It's helpful to have an individual interview with each member of your team that is moving on to offer them feedback and support for the future. If you can't do this make sure someone is on hand who can. If you're lucky enough to have HR people, use them.

It's very helpful if the project manager doesn't have to worry about his/her own career at this stage but the end of a project can mean the end of a job for them too. This makes dismantling the team a difficult job but still very important.

Self development from a project

Don't miss out on the opportunity to gain something personally from your involvement with this project. Don't feel guilty about it – the organisation has invested a lot of money in you; you owe it to them and to yourself to reflect on your own performance and see what you could do better next time.

If you're feeling brave ask your team and/or ask the sponsor. Both will probably be flattered to be asked and may well offer some good constructive criticism. You need to get them to be blunt, maybe with anonymous comments. It's no good for you if they don't tell you the truth. It might hurt, but then, you don't want any surprises, do you?

Project management software

It is certainly possible to successfully manage a complex project with nothing more than pencil and paper – that's how we used to work 25 years ago. Now there are a multitude of software tools available.

The obvious tool for a bigger project is the PC (or Mac – let's not take sides here). Put "project management software" into Google and you'll get many millions of pages so there's clearly lots of it.

Each package has its good points and many have bad points. You can get software that runs on mainframes, desktop computers, laptops and even handhelds.

Whatever software you use, don't trust it and don't rely on it.

It may sound a bit trite to say this but remember that the software doesn't do the work for you. All it really does is take some of the drudgery out of it. You still need to make the decisions.

When you buy software that isn't the end of the cost – there's support and upgrades. Upgrades you may be able to do without but you'll have support costs without any doubt at all.

You need a structured approach to project management without software. With software a structured approach is just as important. You also need to understand the software you're using.

Finally, you must know what you're doing in the first place. Remember the classic computer saying;

GIGO: Garbage In – Garbage Out

This is a succinct way of telling you that if you put incorrect or incomplete data into a machine it will blindly do the calculations and give you its best shot at an answer. A human being might look at the data and know that it made no sense. We haven't yet developed machines that can do this so my philosophy is that you must know how to do all this manually, for then you have a much better chance of spotting when the computer churns out twaddle.

Software products

The most obvious package for PC users is Microsoft Project. The choice is less clear for Mac users as MSP doesn't run under OSX. If you're an Apple fan and want to run MSP, you're going to need to get Windows on your Mac[18]. MS Project covers most requirements of most people and it has the significant advantage that loads of people use it, so you can exchange data easily, but please don't just rush out and buy it. There are a huge number of products out there and the list is constantly changing. It might be worth looking at an alternative.

The trick is to select the one that meets your needs. Decide what sorts of features you want and then look around. Most suppliers will give you demo discs or allow you to download a demo package so you can play with the product and see what the glossy brochure doesn't

---

[18] How? It's not in the book as the products change too fast – check www.3rdsectorskills.com

100

say. Play with it; look at how easy it is to use. Does it work the way you and/or your organisation works? Is it the right scale? By this I mean don't get a product designed for the likes of ICI if you are a small organisation and vice versa. What sort of reports does the software generate? Look at the written reports and the scheduling reports.

Reports

As a project manager you will need to produce reports - for your management, for your customer, and for your team. It's only worth getting the software if it makes your life easier.

If you are running a small project you may be tempted to manage with the standard Office type software. I have seen Gannt charts produced with Excel and Word. But the effort required to persuade Excel or Word to produce readable charts is enormous. When you look at how much it costs to buy real project management software, it's almost certainly worthwhile.

Why would you want to go to the trouble of getting project management software just to draw pretty pictures? You've just answered the question. Gannt charts are easy to produce using real software, they don't take ages and they look professional so they will make you look good to your funders. Plus, as things change through the life of the project it's much, much easier to change the plan if you use real software rather than sledge-hammering Excel.

Software is expensive?

It is if you buy it retail. But as a charity you have access to large discounts if you know where to look. Because written material goes out of date as soon as it's printed I've put links to cheap (and legal) software on the website[19]. Please use them.

Software saves time?

This can be true but it's not always. Software does make your life easier in some respects but there is an overhead. My wife has likened software to a husband – you have to keep feeding it if you want it to do any work. Can't think what she means...

Once you are committed to a software package you are also committed to a machine, and a machine is worse than a husband!

To get good results out of a software package you first need to know how to use it. If you're going to use the same package for more than one project I urge you to get properly trained. It is worth it. There are some excellent training packages out there and they are great to get you started. There's no better teacher than experience, so if you're struggling, get someone who's done it before to come and help for a couple of days. It will be time and money well spent.

Once you know how to use it in general you will need time to bend it to your will – to tweak the calendars and resources to give you better information and help you manage your projects better. And *then* you need to keep it fed with the latest data on a regular basis.

Having put all these obstacles in your path let me say that software can be wonderful, and a great time saver in all sorts of ways.

Software's trump card

The best thing about software is when you need to re-plan. You can move things around and see what effect they have, then go back to the beginning and try something else. You

---

[19] www.3rdsectorskills.com

can see what would happen if situation X were to arise. And 5 minutes later you can do the same for situation Y.

Don't plan at the computer

Please don't fall into the trap of planning at the computer. It's really tempting to sit down and start inputting data into the machine but believe me, for anything other than a really small project (less than 10 tasks) it's courting disaster.

Planning at the machine tends to blinker you and you lose sight of links and dependencies that can really hurt you later on. It is far, far better to adopt the yellow sticky method until you are sure your network is right, then put it on the machine.

Software features

Most of the software packages are absolutely packed with features. If you were to input all the data that they allow you would need two or three full time people for the simplest project. For example, the latest version of Microsoft Project holds more than 300 pieces of data for every single task in your project.

It's very easy to get tied up in the exciting things a piece of software can do. But I have never known anyone who uses all the features in a piece of software. You can do a decent job using about 10% of the facilities. The smart project manager uses the software as a tool and only uses the bits of the tool that are relevant to him/her. If you have a complex project and your organisation has a perfectly adequate method for recording spend, there seems little need to put costs on each task in the software. It's unnecessary fuss and bother. But if your cost collection system is lacking then you might consider using the software to collect your costs.

Data security

BACK UP YOUR DATA

A cautionary tale

Once upon a time there was a project manager who was running a project which involved several suppliers in several countries upgrading a computer system. It was a large and complex project with operations at several locations.

The project plan was on a laptop, allegedly backed up daily by the IT department.

One day the hard disc crashed. IT confessed that their backup hadn't run for several days. Disaster? Fortunately no, because the project manager was a gadget freak and had a £10 piece of software on his Psion 5 palmtop into which he had copied the project plan just for a bit of fun.

The Psion had the only up-to-date copy of the plan and when the laptop broke again, the project manager successfully ran the rest of the project from his palmtop.

The moral of the story is: _don't trust IT (kit or departments)!_ It's true that computer hardware is a lot more reliable today that it used to be but it can still fail or get stolen. _You_ make sure you back up your plan – put it on another computer, on your PDA, or a CD (CDs cost pence – how much is your data worth?) and keep the backup safe. It's just another risk to your project but one you can very easily reduce. So **always** back up your data.

If your project is particularly important to you or to your organisation you might even consider making two copies of your backup and keep one off-site – at home with you for example.

An organisation I know operates out of three sites. They have a policy of backing up each site's data and then storing it at a different site. This way if one site loses data through theft or fire or whatever it is relatively easy to rebuild it at one of the other sites, and their operation is up and running again fairly quickly.

Your PC cost your organisation a few hundred pounds and can easily be replaced. Your data is priceless and could be impossible to replace.

How to backup

There are lots of backup utilities around, some even free. Don't ignore the computer press. There are some really good programs given away free on the cover discs. There is also good software given away when you buy an external hard drive. The important thing is to think about your regime and then stick to it. You may consider using one of the many automatic backup facilities around to back up all your user data daily and store it somewhere sensible. These programs work in the background on your machine and back up your data away to a remote server. It's all encrypted so it's pretty safe and you don't have to worry about remembering to do anything. On the down side you have no control over the company storing your data and if it goes bust your data might go with it. Also the automatic program can slow your machine down if you're not careful.

Whatever you do don't store your backup data on the same disc or the same computer as the original. If you do, you have no protection against a disc crash or damage to, or theft of, the disc. At the very least put your backup on a different disc drive. If you can get your backup off site, so much the better. Make incremental backups so that you don't use acres of disk space, but from time to time run a full backup of everything. Take this backup off site.

I am a Mac user and I use their built-in Time Machine program to keep a copy of my data on an external disc. This copy is made every hour, then consolidated every day so it doesn't use acres of disc. Every day I make an incremental backup of all my company critical data to Apple's online system. That way my really important data is stored on the backup disc and in California. If the big earthquake comes I've got a copy. If my discs die I've got a copy. The daily backup runs at 3 a.m., so I'm rarely bothered by it.

And finally, every now and again I do a backup of the important stuff to a DVD and give it to my sister to keep at her house. I think I've covered all the possibilities and it works for me. Finally, from time to time I review the system and see if I can poke any holes in it.

Do something similar and do it NOW!

A word of warning about CDs & DVDs

CDs and/or DVDs don't last for ever, especially if they're burnt from a PC or Mac. If your data needs to be kept for a long period it's worth reading it off the disc onto your computer every year or so and re-burning a new copy.

Memory sticks

These are great because they're small and hold lots and lots of data. And that's also their biggest weakness. Because they're small, they are very easy to lose. And they are pretty fragile too. They're great for transporting data, but hopeless as a long-term archive medium.

Restoring data

A colleague told me a cautionary tale about a company that dealt in financial data for many thousands of clients. They had a backup system that they considered foolproof and used it carefully. One day some bright spark thought it would be useful to simulate a restore just to prove they could do it, and when they restored a backup they found it was empty! And so were all the other alleged backups! The IT boys got on the case and found that the script they used to do the backup was missing one simple command which was to write the data to the backup medium. Everything else was fine but the data was never written.

The moral of the story is: *when you have your backup routine sorted out try to restore a file or two to make sure you can.*

Working with large projects

What is a large project? The definition varies from organisation to organisation, but a good definition could be that a large project involves a large financial commitment, or a large part of your organisation's resources, or will take a long time, or a combination of all three. However you define it, a large project is more likely to attract the interest of the senior management, trustees, the general public, etc. If it goes wrong it has the potential to damage the organisation, but if it goes well could bring a great deal of benefit.

For all those reasons the spotlight will be on you as project manager so you need to shape up!

To run a large project you need everything you had for a small project but more of it. You will need to be more formal, because if you have more people involved you will need to ensure they all know what the project processes are, and you can't rely on the systems you used for small teams. The only practical way is to write stuff down in a formal way.

Impact on the project manager

If you're a typical third sector project manager looking after smaller projects, it's pretty likely that project management will only be part of your job. You may even manage the project for part of the time and do the actual project work the rest of the time.

But if you're managing a large project, then you (and your organisation) must accept that you'll spend a lot more time, maybe even all of your time, managing the project, and you may not have any left for doing any of the project work. This can be hard to accept sometimes, and you may feel that by 'just' managing the project you're not contributing to the organisation. Be assured that you are. If it's a big project then it needs someone dedicated to making sure it comes in on time, on budget, and delivers what it was supposed to deliver. That's your job.

New things to consider when you have a large project

The processes you need for a large project need to be more formal, because the scale is such that you won't be able to rely on the sort of informality that can work for a smaller project. Paperwork is unfortunately essential when you're running a big project. You need to ensure that all of the project team know what they are supposed to be doing and how the project is getting on. If your team is small and all located in the same place, then it's quite easy. If you have a large team scattered around the countryside, you need to be a lot more careful.

You will have a lot more data to collect and unless you have good processes in place it will be all too easy to lose information, which is not good.

As with small projects you *still* must have a

- project brief
- project plan
- risk log/register
- issue report log/register

And you now need

- A formal system for issue reporting and logging
- A formal system for risk analysis and logging
- A formal system for change requests and control

Again, what follows works. You need to decide if the level of complexity merits it for your project. How much of this you use is up to you.

Opportunities and Threats

The processes for identifying opportunities and threats are basically the same regardless of the size of the project. The difference is that if you are running a large project there are usually more of them and they're bigger! You can use the techniques described earlier to deal with them but, because of the numbers involved you will need to be more formal about the process to deal with them, to identify and log them, and to record the actions you are taking to minimise them.

Risk and contingency planning

We covered risk earlier in this book and there is little to add except that bigger projects usually carry bigger risks and there are usually more of them.

Risks that are peculiar to large projects include:

- communication difficulties due to having a larger team and keeping that team focused;

- a team that is spread over a wider geographical area – how do you ensure things are happening when they're supposed to? What processes do you have in place to ensure you have no surprises?

- a larger chunk of the organisation's resources;

- a higher profile, both inside and outside the organisation.

It might be a good idea to hold special risk review meetings and involve people from other parts of the organisation to attend. That way you can be (more) certain that all the risks have been adequately identified and appropriate steps taken to minimise them.

Project Team

The heart of good project management is ensuring your whole team is working towards the same goal, that they each understand their part in the process, and that you monitor progress closely.

With a large project it is more likely that your team will be bigger and more geographically diverse which means you will have to give a lot more thought and expend a lot more energy holding your team together. A properly thought-out communication plan is really important, as are well thought-out control mechanisms.

Communications

As soon as your team is too big to fit in a single office the communications problems start to grow. When that team is spread over a number of locations you have to give a good deal of thought to how you can ensure all the members of the team receive the communications they need.

There are ways to make this less difficult but in my opinion nothing beats a face-to-face meeting. If you can, have a full face-to-face team meeting at or near the start of the project. This helps to establish some team spirit and at least people know what their fellow team members look like. If possible continue to have regular face-to-face meetings, but if this is not practicable then you will need to use some of the alternatives discussed earlier. It's really important that keeping your team involved doesn't end up on the 'too difficult pile' just because they are remote from your office.

Planning

A large project suggests a large project plan. If your plan has many tasks it is easy to get lost in the middle of a pile of paper unsure of which task links to which – all those lines look the same.

It can be very useful to split your project into a number of smaller stages and treat each stage as a sub-project. This approach makes it easier to manage and also gives the organisation the opportunity to thoroughly review the project at the end of each stage.

It makes sense to put together a top-level plan to cover the whole project, then plan each stage in detail at an appropriate time. Consider a 2 year project which you've split into 4 or 5 stages. You will certainly need an overall plan for the whole project, but it probably doesn't make sense to plan stage 5 in detail at the beginning. Much could change in the next 18 months, so it might be better to leave detailed planning until your project has been going for a while. When you do plan stage 5 you'll have the benefit of knowing what has happened so far.

Another use for stages is to give the organisation the opportunity to conduct a thorough review at the end of each stage. The external environment may change over the 2 years, and it might be that after 18 months the reason for implementing the project has gone away. The formal review gives you the opportunity to stop the project rather than just carry on for the sake of it.

If you have a large project to manage, it is probably worth investing in some software – it will make it easier to keep track of a large number of tasks.

Aside – I once worked with an organisation with a rule about big plans. If the plan doesn't fit on one side of A4 (with a font big enough to read easily!) then split it into sub-projects. That may be a little extreme, but it worked for them.

Keeping track of problems

With a larger project, and possibly more people involved, the need to keep a written log of problems and issues is even greater. The more people you have to deal with the more possibilities there are for misunderstandings.

Some problems can be dealt with instantly. But others need to be passed to someone else, or thought about, or parked until the appropriate time. It's really important that these do not get lost. Keep a log of all the issues including who is responsible for clearing them up. Clearly all issues aren't equally important – the showstoppers need immediate action, but you can keep the minor issues to one side and clear them all up together.

Despite my loathing of paperwork I strongly advise you write all issues down in a log. A seemingly minor issue can develop into a real problem if it's forgotten.

Project issues

Regard EVERY problem as an issue to be addressed. Insist that every project member raise an "Issue Report" whenever he/she is unsure about something, notices a problem, or has an idea about the project. This could be serious or trivial, but it's important that all uncertainty is sorted out.

Examples

- Computer order does not specify size of monitor (can't decide straight away, have to ask customer which he prefers and check prices)
- Handbook for process is incorrect (need the process owner to correct it)
- If we were to approach this task in *this* way, we could save time/money

An issue report is a note of something that is not quite right.

You must have a process to deal with project issues. Each issue must be recorded and given a unique number. In this way none can be lost. Once the issue is recorded some time has to be given to consider it and some action taken. The decision should be recorded with the original issue, and the originator informed of the action.

It is really useful to have a special form for dealing with issues and a good trick is to print this form on coloured paper, which makes it very difficult to lose. The form does not have to be complex, just enough to hold the relevant information. There's a template available on the website.

Once you have an issue you need to consider what it means. How severe is it? You can generally classify them into one of four categories.

- Severity 1 – showstopper
- Severity 2 – Major; important but not yet a showstopper
- Severity 3 – Minor
- Severity 4 – Interesting (!)

Stuart's other golden rule is ...

> *No Issue Report - no problem*

If a problem doesn't have an issue number it does not exist. Taking this position can make you initially unpopular but making people write down an issue in a formal way has a number of advantages.

- It weeds out the truly trivial problems and those that can be sorted out immediately.
- It makes sure the issue is properly described
- It makes sure that people know what they're talking about when they discuss an issue in the future
- It avoids misunderstandings

This is more suitable to larger projects perhaps but still has value for smaller ones. It's very easy to miss small but important problems if there are bigger ones around. This system makes you think about each issue and whether it really is a problem after all.

It's also a great way to collect a lot of minor points and clear them up in one go, saving time overall.

Issue log

Keep a log of all issues similar to the risk register discussed earlier.

For each issue note

- the number;
- the severity;
- a description of the problem;
- who is assigned to resolve it;
- what is the deadline for a fix.

Keep on top of them; keep chasing them down so they get fixed. There's nothing more irritating than being nagged by a project manager about some little issue for months on end – it's a great way to get motivated to fix it, just for some peace and quiet.

Get them cleared. A small issue log with evidence of actions being taken to clear them is a great document to wave in front of a customer. S/he sees action and is pleased.

Change control

With a large project your chances of having no changes are absolutely zero. It is vital that you have a well-structured change control process. With a small project such a process need not be too formal, but for a large project you need to have a formal method for raising changes, logging them, analysing them, deciding what to do about them, and integrating the new work into the project plan. You, as project manager, must be the final arbiter of changes, as you are responsible for the delivery of the project.

Maintain a change request log

Just as with a smaller project, keep a note of all change requests and what action was agreed. If the change was accepted keep a note of what the implications were and what the customer agreed to. Make sure any changes to the project acceptance criteria are agreed by the customer. You'll need this information when you come to hand over the project, because then you're handing over the original project plus all the changes.

Managing multi-site projects

Get on your bike. You need to get about and visit your outlying people from time to time. Remember that half the job of a project manager is to hold your team together and keep them all happy. You won't do this if they never see you.

You can use all the nice modern methods of communication but nothing beats getting everyone together now and again, if you can afford to do it. The productivity gains are worth the expense.

---

[20] More about this on page 91

Summary

Large projects are like small projects – only bigger!

(That has to take a prize for the most daft thing to say.) The only real difference is likely to be the number of tasks, the number of people and the amount of money involved. You need to be more formally organised if you're running a bigger project, just because you can't hope to keep all the details in your head. There may be one or more project managers working together and so you need to make sure all the information you require is accessible to all of them.

With a bigger team communication needs to be better organised. You can't just get the team into your office for a coffee and a chat – you may need to plan project meetings well in advance so people can travel.

The actual project management tasks are not really any different – balancing time, budget and scope are still there.

Don't be put off by the size of a project. The challenges may be greater but so is the feeling of achievement when it all comes together.

Working with multiple projects

Many project managers in the voluntary sector work on many projects at once. This has its own share of exciting issues. Some of these are

- how do you keep on top of all these projects?
- how do you manage people that may be working on several projects at any one time?
- how do you juggle priorities between projects?

This book is long enough already. To go into detail on juggling multiple projects would make it too heavy to lift, so I will mention briefly some of the big issues.

Keeping on top of multiple projects

Well the good news is that (usually) projects aren't all at crisis point at the same time, so you can (usually) let some just get on with themselves, while devoting your attention to one or two that need work.

It's a variation of the 80/20 rule.

Having said that, there is no substitute for careful planning and working hard to keep on top of things. Getting your project teams to keep you up to date with progress and highlight any issues coming their way is a good discipline; it means that you can presume that everything is ok unless you've been told otherwise. But, and it's a big but, you need to make sure you check that everything really IS ok.

Careful planning is a theme which will be repeated in this section, but if you're handling multiple projects you need them to be carefully planned and carefully monitored. If nothing else, you need to be sure that you're not required in London for a project meeting with a funder on the same day that another funder is expecting you in Newcastle. That's a simple example, but it makes the point.

Managing people

It's likely that you'll have people who will be working on more than one project. This can be tough, because they may have their own ideas about what's most important and they may not always agree with you. However, you need to make it clear what tasks have the highest priority, and why. That last point is crucial – I've found that explaining why is the biggest help to getting people to do what you want them to do.

You need to have a decent project planning tool that can cope with one resource being allocated to more than one project. This is where software really comes into its own, but this is also where you need to know what you're doing with the software. Get trained in how to use it. Resources and resource allocation is one area where a little knowledge is really dangerous.

When you're managing people who work on more than one of your projects you will come up against conflicting priorities; read on...

Juggling priorities

With a little luck, you will know what the priorities are in your organisation and so it shouldn't be too hard to translate that into the priorities amongst your multiple projects. But life is rarely so kind; one day you will come up against it and find that one project has to give because you have two things to do, and can only do one of them.

You are likely to be faced with people all demanding that their project is the most important. But this is where it's useful to be managing several projects, because you will have an idea of the other project plans in your head. Remember some pages ago I talked about the project manager being the only person to have sight of the whole picture? This is especially true when you are talking about multiple projects. The people clamouring for their pet project are unlikely to have sight of the whole picture, and so you will be the best person to judge which project you will allow to slip today. You will make that decision knowing what options the other projects have to make up time, or lose a little scope or whatever. When I have been faced with this sort of decision, I tried to think of the big picture and make the decision according to the bigger needs of the organisation. It was a case of 'we need to win the war so we can afford to lose the odd battle'.

It's fun

It's fun working with multiple projects, because there's never time to get bored and you can see the organisation moving forward on many fronts at the same time. It makes for an "interesting life", but it's really rewarding.

What Can Go Wrong

The purpose of this book is to help you NOT to go wrong. It's still worth knowing why projects do go wrong.

It is a sobering thought that 25% of projects fail. And 1 project in 3 that 'succeeds' (i.e. is delivered on time, on budget and on scope) fails to deliver the expected value to the organisation; "gosh, it was a great project, but we still have the problem it was supposed to fix – oops".

A project fails for many reasons. It doesn't seem to matter what the project is, which sector it's in, or how big it is, the top five reasons for failure are the same. They are:-

- Team unsure of project objectives
- Team unsure of project deliverables
- At the end of the project, the objectives were only partially met
- The planned schedule tended to run late
- The budget was exceeded

I'm being particularly harsh with my definition of failure. If a project misses a single objective even by a hair's breadth, it's failed. By this definition the project can be a roaring success to the outside world but still 'failed' internally.

Look at the above list and think about it.

Unsure of objectives/deliverables

The first two reasons for failure are, without any doubt at all, your fault. If your team don't know what they're supposed to be doing, how can they possibly succeed? Ditto on the deliverables. How can they succeed if they don't know what they're supposed to deliver? You're on a loser from day one.

If any of your team aren't sure of something, I'm afraid that's your fault. Communicating clear objectives and deliverables to your team is part of your job, a really important part of your job. And no-one else can take the rap for not doing it. Sorry, but that's the way it is.

The next 3 reasons may also be your fault but you may be forgiven for some of them.

Nearly met objectives

The third reason is probably the most common. You almost succeeded, delivered most of the objectives, but not all. Remember when you set out these objectives, it was crystal ball time. You were looking into the future and making a judgement on what you were going to achieve. Now you're at the end of the project, look back and ask yourself: "Was I way too optimistic? Was I way too pessimistic? Did something occur during the lifetime of the project that made the original objectives unattainable? If so, what was it?"

There is a good case for reviewing the project objectives at stages during the project life cycle and, if necessary, revising them.

Ran late/exceeded budget

There are a number of reasons why the project could run late. The estimates could have been wrong to start with, your resource might not have been good enough, external factors took resource away, and so on.

Did you forget something when you did the budget? Did you underestimate the resources required for some tasks? Did something external happen (like the price of oil shooting through the roof)?

--- ☆ ☆ ☆ ---

We can all come up with good reasons (excuses) for failing but most of them are down to poor project management. Following the guidelines in this book will not guarantee you success but you will increase your chances of avoiding failure. Projects are risky and so there is no guarantee of success, but there are tried and tested techniques to give you the best chance.

By far the most important thing to do is to understand what the project has to deliver and to make sure that _everybody_ associated with the project shares the same understanding. That's half the battle.

What next?

Learning project management from a book is like learning to ride a bicycle by reading a book. You can learn all the theory you like but you need to do it.

So go forth and manage.

Project management is a personal thing. We each have our own styles but we all use (or should use) the same fundamental techniques. Use the techniques from this book and if they work for you, carry on using them. If they don't quite gel, then modify them according to your way of working.

--- ☆ ☆ ☆ ---

Read more. There are millions (ok, thousands, it just seems like millions) of project management books out there. They all teach more or less the same thing but in different ways. In my experience many of them concentrate solely on the processes and neglect the people part. My view is that anyone can construct a project plan and produce a pretty Gannt chart, but that's only half the story. The tools are just tools. The art of project management lies in the people skills.

Consider joining a professional organisation such as the Association of Project Managers or the Project Management Institute. They have journals and special interest groups where you can keep up with the latest thinking.

There are plenty of forums on the internet, and networking sites with special interest groups.

--- ☆ ☆ ☆ ---

But above all, have fun. Project management *is* fun! There are few better feelings than sitting back at the end of a project and knowing that you changed the world. It may be only a small change but nevertheless the world is different now, and hopefully your client group will be better off as a result. That's a nice feeling.

HAVE FUN!

Appendix 1 – Exercises

In this Appendix you'll find some exercise sheets. If you don't fancy messing up this book, you can go to www.3rdsectorskills.com and download all of these sheets in pdf format so you can have lots of fun, again and again!

Objectives

Use this sheet to construct objectives, then tick off the SMART columns

No.		S	M	A	R	T
1						
2						
3						
4						
5						
6						

Risks

Use this sheet to identify project risks, then assign them a probability & impact

Description of risk	Prob.			Impact		
	Low	Medium	High	Low	Medium	High

Risk Register

Take each risk, then write down the action you will take to minimise it

No.	Risk	Impact	Prob.	Action

Decorating a room – task list

Take these tasks, ignore the durations for now, and put together a network showing which tasks are dependent.

Don't turn to the next page – it shows my version of the network, and that would be cheating!

Task No	Description	Duration (days)
1	Buy wallpaper	1
2	Buy paint (woodwork)	1
3	Buy paint (ceiling)	1
4	Wash ceiling	1
5	Paint ceiling	1
6	Paint woodwork	2
7	Empty room	1
8	Refill room	2
9	Strip wallpaper	2
10	Hang wallpaper	2
11	Prepare woodwork	2

Don't expect to get the same network as I did. There are many ways to put this project together, depending on the way you do your decorating. The important thing is not to put any dependencies in your network that aren't necessary in the real world.

Once you've finished, you can look at the network I came up with, which is on the next page. Put the durations into the various tasks, then work out the critical path. It's straightforward as long as there is only one link in and one link out of each task. Whenever there's more than one, you will need to check all the incoming tasks.

You can find the answer in Appendix 5.

Decorating a room – network diagram

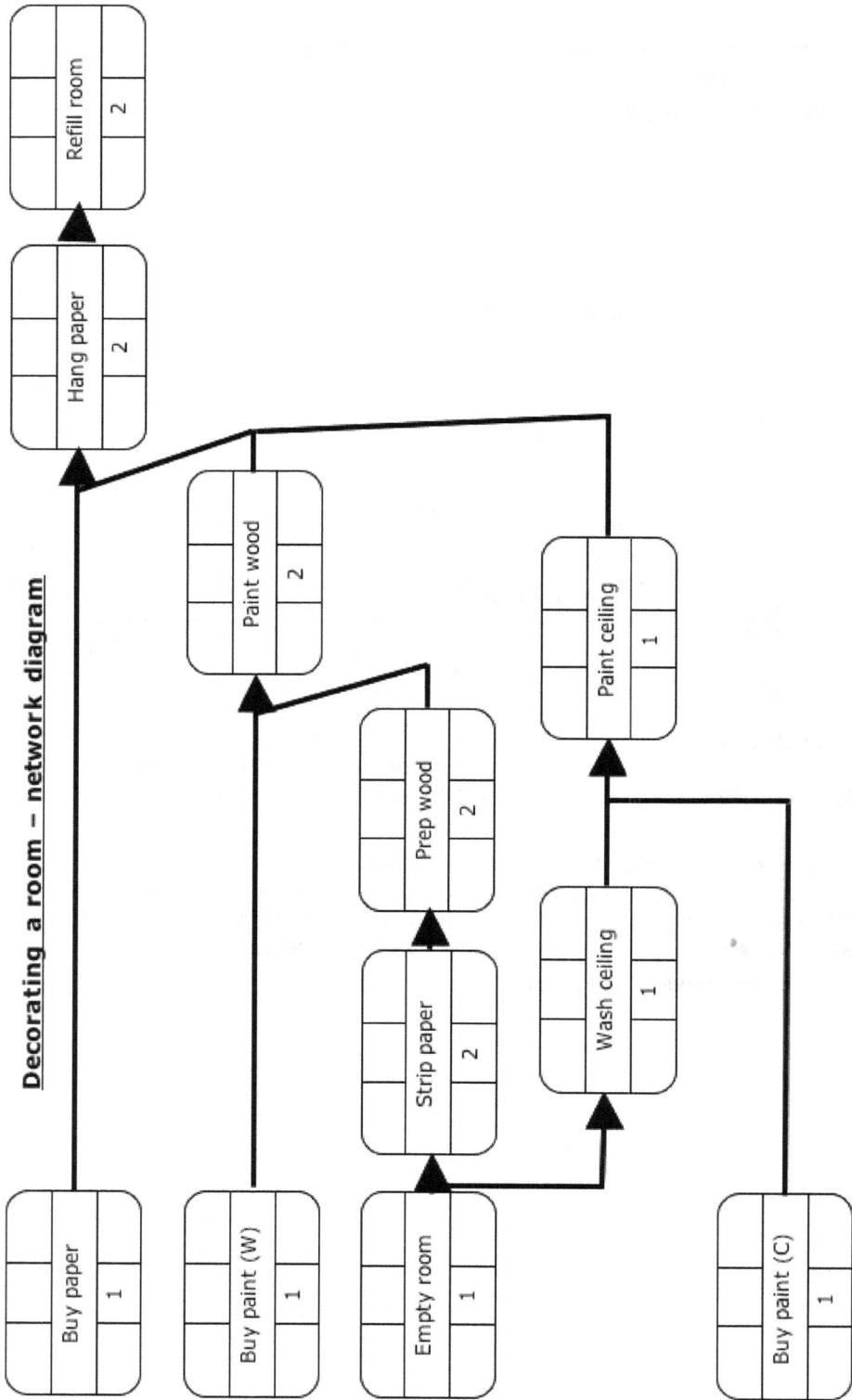

	Refill room	
		2

	Hang paper	
		2

	Paint wood	
		2

	Prep wood	
		2

	Paint ceiling	
		1

	Buy paper	
		1

	Buy paint (W)	
		1

	Strip paper	
		2

	Empty room	
		1

	Wash ceiling	
		1

	Buy paint (C)	
		1

Appendix 2 – Discounted Cash Flow

Discounted cash flow calculations are carried out routinely in commercial organisations where a return on investment is required. But these calculations are valid in voluntary organisations as well. Charities, too, get involved in projects that must demonstrate a return. Even if you're not looking for a return on investment, it's still worth doing the calculations. If nothing else, the results will give the senior management or trustees a clear picture of the financial impact of the project on their organisation, and they will then be in a better position to judge whether the project is worthwhile or not.

The calculations yield the payback period, which is the period of time it takes until the project shows a positive return to the organisation, and the size of the return.

An example

The best way to understand the process is to work through an example. Suppose your trustees have just decided that the boiler in the office is too costly to run and they want you to look into replacing it.

You naturally carry out a financial appraisal for this project before you agree.

The facts

At the moment, the boiler costs £200 per year in fuel and £80 per year in maintenance. Your heating man tells you that a new boiler will cost you £400 to install but will use less fuel than at present, about £150 per year. In addition, it comes with a 2 year guarantee and after that annual maintenance will only cost £60 per year. On top of that(!), your existing boiler is getting old and is likely to cost more like £100 per year to maintain from next year.

Example 1 – simple method

With this method, you construct a table showing the cashflow over the length of the project.

Year	2011	2012	2013	2014	2015	
Old boiler						
Fuel	200	200	200	200	200	
Maintenance	80	100	100	100	100	
Total	280	300	300	300	300	Row A
Cumulative	280	580	880	1180	1480	
New boiler						
Installation	400					
Fuel	150	150	150	150	150	
Maintenance			60	60	60	
Total	550	150	210	210	210	Row B
Cumulative	550	700	910	1120	1330	
Assume new boiler installed, then...						
Annual cash saving/(loss)	(270)	150	90	90	90	A-B
Cumulative cash saving/(loss)	(270)	(120)	(30)	60	**150**	

Table 2 - Simple cashflow calculation

Table 2 shows the cashflow for each boiler over the next 5 years. Note that if a number has a bracket around it, it means bad news; so in 2011, the cashflow is negative, which means the organisation is out of pocket to the tune of £270.

For the old boiler, I put in the fuel cost in each year and then the maintenance costs (as far as we know them). Adding these gave the total cost of the boiler in each of the 5 years. Just for fun (!) I added the years together to get the cumulative cost over the period, which shows that the old boiler will cost us £1480 over 5 years.

I did the same sort of thing for the new boiler, remembering to add in the £400 installation costs in the first year. The cumulative cost of the new boiler is only £1330, which suggests we're onto a winner already.

But when does the organisation recover from the £400 installation cost? We need to work out the *net cashflow*, if we put in the new boiler. To do this, we take the cost of the new boiler away from the cost of the old boiler, year by year. We take row B numbers away from row A numbers.

So in the first year the new boiler costs the organisation £270 more than the old one. In the second year we're £150 better off, and so it continues. By working out the cumulative net costs, we see that overall the organisation is worse off for the first couple of years, but by the end of 2014, we are in pocket. The whole project breaks even sometime in 2014, and from then on the cumulative effect is to save the organisation money.

The payback period is said to be between 2 and 3 years (because the first year is traditionally called year zero, and so 2012 is year 1, 2013 year 2, etc).

If we want a more accurate figure for payback, we can plot the figures on a graph, or get Microsoft to do it for us. (Excel has a neat little function that will do all this maths for us.) Figure 33 shows the payback is about 2.3 years.

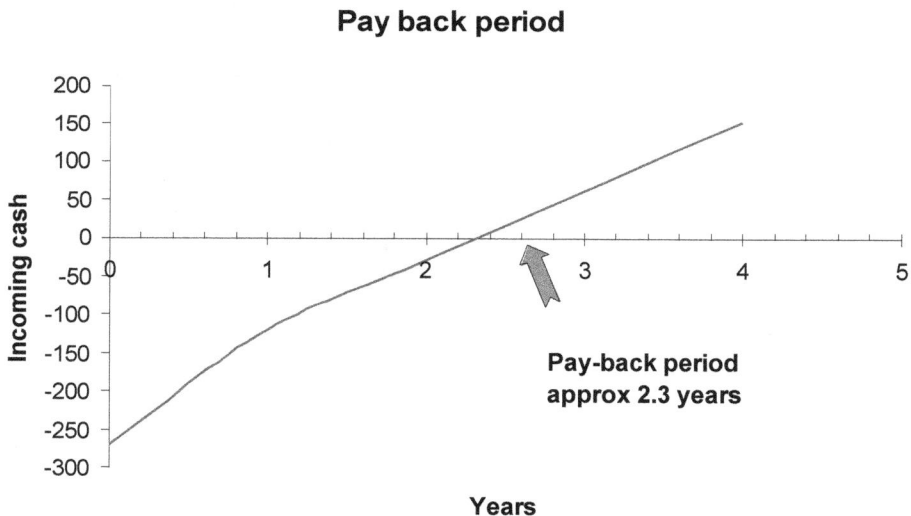

Figure 33 – Payback period

Assumptions

Note that this whole approach is riddled with assumptions, and it's really important that we know what those assumptions are and they are included them in our proposal. For example

124

we've assumed that the price of fuel will remain static over the lifetime of the project. We've also assumed that the maintenance cost will not change over time, etc.

Conclusion

So our calculations show that over the 5 year life of the project, the total money saved by the new boiler is £150 and it will save running costs in 2012, but the whole project will not break even until about a third of the way through 2014.

It looks as though we're in a position to make some useful decisions now. It seems worthwhile replacing the boiler, but not if our lease runs out in 2013, because by then the project will not yet have broken even.

But....

Sorry, but that information isn't completely accurate.

The problem with the simple method used above is that it does not take into account the fact that £1 earned or spent in the future has less value than £1 earned or spent today. To take account of this, we have to get involved with discounted cash flow, which sounds fearsome but isn't.

Discounted Cash Flow made easy (!)

Suppose interest rates are 10%. If someone offered you £100 today, or £100 in one year's time, which would you take? Most of us would take the money now because

- we can spend it now;
- if we wait for a year and then spend it we won't be able to buy so much with it because inflation will have put prices up. In order to have the same spending power, we would need to have £100 plus £x, where x represents the increase in prices over the year;
- there's the chance that the person offering the money won't be around in a year's time, so we'd look pretty stupid if we waited;
- if we had the £100 now we might be able to invest it and earn interest on it.

If the interest rate is 10%, then in order to have the purchasing power of today's £100 in a year's time, we need to have £100 plus 10% or £110 at that future time. In this example, £100 today is equivalent to £110 in a year's time. In accountant-speak, £100 is the *present value* of £110 in one year's time, at a *discount rate* of 10%. Note that the present value is a lower number than the value in a year's time, the future value.

When we constructed the cashflow table earlier, we had different amounts of money being spent/received at different times in the future. How can we make a truly informed decision on the true cost of the project? If we could bring all those different amounts, at different times, back to their present values, we could take the time differences away and we could make a proper decision.

It can be done, and it's not difficult.

Discount rate

The first thing we must have is a number to describe the rate at which money changes value. This number is called the discount rate, and it takes into account all sorts of factors that affect the value of money. Essentially it's based on the rate of return we might expect if we invested the money instead of spending it. It stems from the commercial sector where people take rate of return very seriously.

For most projects, taking the discount rate as the rate of inflation is good enough. An obvious exception would be if you're in the housing business when are dealing with mortgage rates and suchlike. If this is you, then get some informed advice about which rate to use.

Once we have your discount rate, you can then work out the future and present values you need to make your informed decision.

Here is the maths

If numbers do nothing for you, then skip this section and go straight to Example 2 on page 127. If you want to know where the numbers come from, then the next page or so is for you.

The question we need to answer is "if we need, say, £100 in a year's time, how much do we need today to generate £100 in a year's time?" Alternatively, "if we're going to receive £100 in a year's time, how much would that be worth if we received it today?"

Just for now, let's assume that the discount rate we're using is 10%. (Depending on when you read this book this will either be ludicrously high, or ludicrously low. Never mind, let's go with it.)

Going back to our earlier sum we saw that

$$£100 \ in \ a \ year = £Some \ value + (£Some \ value \times 10\%)$$

Let's be a little more professional and replace "Some value" and "£100 in a year" with the proper terms, which are "present value" and "future value" respectively. So the equation now becomes

$$Future \ Value = Present \ Value + (Present \ value \times 10\%).$$

A little bit of elementary algebra and we can simplify this to

$$Future \ Value = Present \ Value \times (1 + Discount \ Rate)$$

and then we re-arrange the formula to give

$$Present \ Value = \frac{Future \ Value}{(1 + Discount \ Rate)}$$

and we can use this formula to work out the present value if we know the future value and the discount rate. This is very nearly the formula that we use most of the time, but we can make it just a little bit easier still.

Discount rate and discount factor

If you think back to your Maths 'O' level, or GCSE, you should remember that division and multiplication are related. So, to make life easy for ourselves, we don't use the quantity (1+discount rate) because that involves division, but rather a quantity called the discount factor.

$$Discount \ Factor = \frac{1}{(1 + Discount \ Rate)}$$

which means we can now write

$$Present \ Value = Future \ Value \times Discount \ Factor$$

and that's much simpler.

In the example we're looking at the discount rate is 10% (which is 0.1) and so the discount factor is

$$Discount \ Factor = \frac{1}{(1 + 0.1)} = \frac{1}{1.1} = 0.909$$

and so we can see that

$$Present\ Value = Future\ Value \times 0.909.$$

That's all very well for one year, but usually we're interested in more than one year. This is where the maths gets a tiny bit more complex. For the second year we need to multiply by the discount factor again.

$$Present\ Value = (Future\ Value \times Discount\ Factor) \times Discount\ Factor$$

or

$$Present\ Value = Future\ Value \times Discount\ Factor^2$$

And for three years the formula is

$$Present\ Value = Future\ Value \times Discount\ Factor^3$$

The formula for working it out for any number of years is

$$Present\ Value = Future\ Value \times Discount\ Factor^n$$

where 'n' is the number of years.

Harking back again to your maths lessons, that 'n' just means multiply discount factor by itself *n* times.

You don't have to remember all this, because it has been reduced to a mechanical process by generations of accountants, but it's good to know where the numbers come from. In practice you'll use a look-up table. There's a printed table in Appendix 4 - Table of Discount Factors, or you can download a bigger version in Excel from the website[21].

It's all a lot clearer if we look at a practical example, so let's go back to the boiler example and see how it all works in practice.

Example 2 - Discounted Cash Flow

In the boiler example we worked out the net cashflow for each year from 2011 until 2015.

Year	2011	2012	2013	2014	2015
Net cashflow: saving/(loss)	(270)	150	90	90	90

Table 3 - Net cashflow for simple calculation

We now know that, for example, the £90 net saving in 2013 isn't worth £90 at today's values. We need to bring all those future values back to the present to see how much the boiler will cost in today's terms.

Let's assume that the discount rate is 10%, because it's nice and easy.

We're starting off in in 2011, so that loss of £270 is already at today's value.

For year 1 (2012) we need to go to the table in Appendix 4 - Table of Discount Factors and find the column headed 10%. Go down the column until we get to the row for year 1, and where they intersect is the discount factor, which is 0.909.

The present value is simply the cash saving (£150) multiplied by 0.909, which is £136.

We'll ignore the pennies, because, with all the assumptions built-in to the discount rate, the pounds value alone is close enough. It's interesting to see that it's quite a lot less than £150.

---

[21] www.3rdsectorskills.com

In a similar way we can calculate the present value of the cash saving in year 2 (2013). Use the table to find the discount factor, which in this case, is 0.826. Multiply £90 by 0.826 to get a present value of £74.

We carry on until the end of the project in year 4 or 2015 and we get a series of present values.

Year	2011	2012	2013	2014	2015
Net cashflow: saving/(loss)	(270)	150	90	90	90
Discount factor	1	0.909	0.826	0.751	0.683
Present value	(270)	136	74	68	61
Cumulative cashflow	(270)	(134)	(60)	8	**69**

Net present value

Table 4 - Present value calculation

The cumulative cashflow over the length of the project is now only £69.

This is interesting. This method shows that the total money saved over the 5 years, at today's values, comes to only £69, compared with the £150 predicted by the simple method. This is because we have now taken the present value of money earned in the future into account.

The value of £69 is called the *net present value, or NPV* of the project. It is effectively saying that the net effect of the project is to bring in £69 at today's values.

There are a number of factors which dictate whether or not you should to go through this exercise. For a small project it is may not worthwhile – the difference in this example is only £81, but it's still more than half the figure we got using the simple method. For a project that calls for a significant investment, or runs over a long time period, it is really essential.

It is pretty obvious that if you appraise the project over a longer period of time, the NPV will be different. So it should also be pretty obvious that you need to take great care in deciding the period you choose. It has to be sensible, and if you are presenting your conclusions to senior management or trustees, you need to include the project life in your report.

It's also clear that if you use a different discount rate, then the NPV will also be different. To illustrate this I've done some more calculations with the same numbers, the same project length, but different discount rates. Figure 34 shows how the NPV of the boiler project varies with varying discount rates. It's clear that at a discount rate of 10% the NPV is about £69. If the discount rate is 15%, we can see from the graph that the NPV is about £40. Is the project still worth doing?

Keep moving along the axis and we come to a point when the NPV becomes negative. This means that the project will not break even, but will lose money over its life. In this case it's when the discount rate is about 23%. Any more than 23% and you'd be better off sticking with the existing boiler.

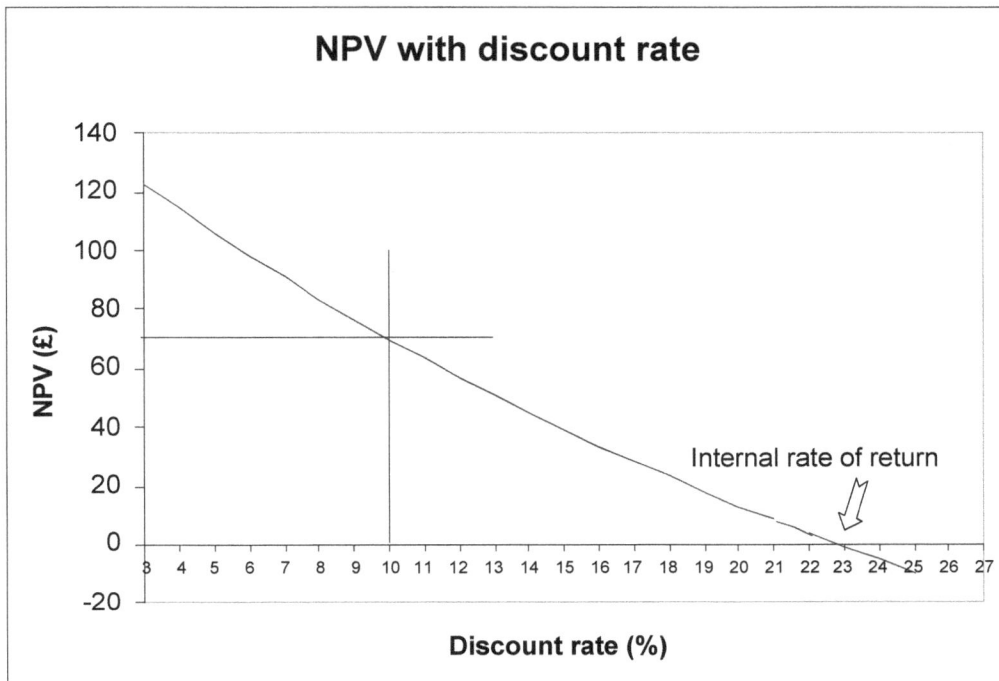

Figure 34 – NPV with discount rate

The point at which the line crosses the x-axis has special significance – it is that value of the discount rate where the project breaks even. It is called the *internal rate of return* of the project. In this case it is just less than 23%.

Internal rate of return (IRR)

The internal rate of return is a means by which you take yet another variable out of the system. No-one can predict the discount rate in the future. Today it might seem sensible to choose a rate of, say, 10%. But a couple of years down the line, who knows what will happen? Interest rates may soar or plummet, so how can you take this into account?

The internal rate of return is one way to take that unpredictability out of the problem. In this example, you can see that unless the discount rate rises above 23%, the project will still give some return. Only if it exceeds 23% will it lose money.

The IRR shows you how big your cushion is. Since you chose 10% as your discount rate you have a pretty big cushion. If, however, your chosen rate was 15% and the IRR turned out to be 20%, it's time to consider some of your options a little more carefully.

This is particularly useful when you have more than one option to assess. Because the whole process takes into account the time at which money becomes available as well as the amount, you can judge more than one option realistically with another.

Compare two options

Let's imagine that there is a second type of boiler available to your organisation. It costs a little less to install, the fuel cost are a little higher, the guarantee is longer but thereafter the maintenance costs are higher. How do you decided between the two options?

Here is the information in tabular form, using the simple method. We'll assume for a moment that the project life stays at 5 years.

Year	2011	2012	2013	2014	2015
Old boiler					
Fuel	200	200	200	200	200
Maintenance	80	100	100	100	100
Total	280	300	300	300	300
Cumulative	280	580	880	1180	1480
New boiler					
Installation	350				
Fuel	160	160	160	160	160
Maintenance				90	90
Total	510	160	160	250	250
Cumulative	510	670	830	1080	1330
Annual cash saving/(loss)	(230)	140	140	50	50
Cumulative cash saving/(loss)	(230)	(90)	50	100	**150**

Table 5 - Simple cashflow calculation: option 2

If you look back to the first example, you'll see that both boilers show the same return using the simple method - this is a cunning ploy to fool you! It shows that using the simple method does not allow you to distinguish between the two options in this case. What will you do? Fortunately, discounted cash flow is galloping to your aid!

Table 6 shows the discounted cashflow calculations for the two options.

Year	Option 1 annual cashflow	Discount rate	Present value	Option 2 annual cashflow	Discount rate	Present value
0	(270)	1	(270)	(230)	1	(230)
1	150	0.909	136	140	0.909	127
2	90	0.826	74	140	0.826	115
3	90	0.751	68	50	0.751	37
4	90	0.683	61	50	0.683	34
NPV			**69**			**83**
IRR			**23%**			**30%**

Table 6 - Comparison of NPVs

The comparative calculations clearly show that the second option has a higher NPV over the 5 year life of the project. This makes sense, because the payback time for option 1 was sometime in 2012, whereas for option 2 it's a year earlier. You can also see that the money coming into the organisation arrives earlier and is in larger amounts earlier in the project life. So the NPV calculations agree with instinct in this case.

The internal rates of return also show that option 2 is the more sensible one to choose.

Of course, this is a very simple example, but the principles apply to any size of project.

IRR and discount rates

In the commercial world, the discount rate you choose against which to appraise a project will be some number conjured up by the finance people. It will take into account the prevailing interest rates, the amount of risk the organisation is prepared to tolerate, and some indication of the minimum return the organisation is prepared to accept in order to deliver the required value to its shareholders.

It is possible that you will meet this kind of thing in your organisation. Although the voluntary sector doesn't have shareholders as such, more and more third sector projects are quasi-commercial – the organisation must look at them from a commercial point of view – and some projects are strictly commercial, for example moving to new premises or installing infra-structure systems. So the need for more formal project appraisal techniques is growing.

No matter what your project, using these techniques will give you a much better idea of its financial cost. Whether you choose to pursue the project depends on many more issues, as we have already discussed.

NPV vs. project life

I mentioned earlier that the NPV depends on not just the discount rate, but also the life of the project. If you were to work out the numbers for a projected 10 year life of the boiler, assuming everything else was equal, then for option 1 the two NPVs are completely different. Figure 35 shows that there's a 12% difference in the IRR for these two projects, and that's considerable by anyone's standards.

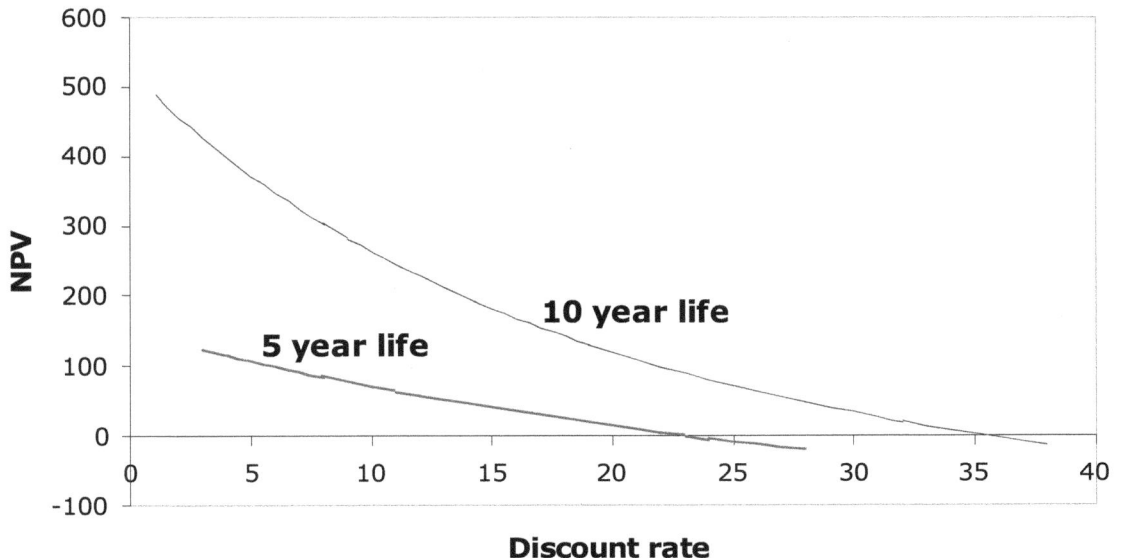

Figure 35 – Internal rate of return for Option 1

Summary

Financial appraisal is not an exact science. You are predicting the discount rate for a number of years, predicting the life of the project, predicting the anticipated income from it, and a number of other factors. That's a lot of predicting. All you can do is make reasonable assumptions (making sure the people who make the decisions know what they are) and do the calculations.

The NPV and IRR are not magic numbers – but if the appraisal is carried out properly, they give you and your management a good indication of the likely financial impact of your project on the organisation.

Appendix 3 – Additional resources

A paper book can only cover so much, and some of it will be out of date in no time.

The 3rd Sector Skills website is devoted to management in the charitable and voluntary sectors and there's lots of good stuff there, especially about project management.

Check the resources pages for downloads, links and more.

For example, you'll find downloadable versions of the next three pages, and if you're really into discounted cashflow there's a bigger version of the spreadsheet.

If there's something you want that you can't find on the site, let us know, and we'll see what we can do – within reason; can't magic an Aston Martin out of thin air!

The next couple of pages show a simple project in Gannt chart and PERT chart format, really just to illustrate the differences between the two representations. The Gannt chart is relatively easy to read and to understand. The PERT chart is for exactly the same project, but is hard to read, mainly because the print has to be so tiny to cram it into those little boxes, and I had to split it at the thick wavy line in order to fit it into one page.

Gannt chart – decorating a room

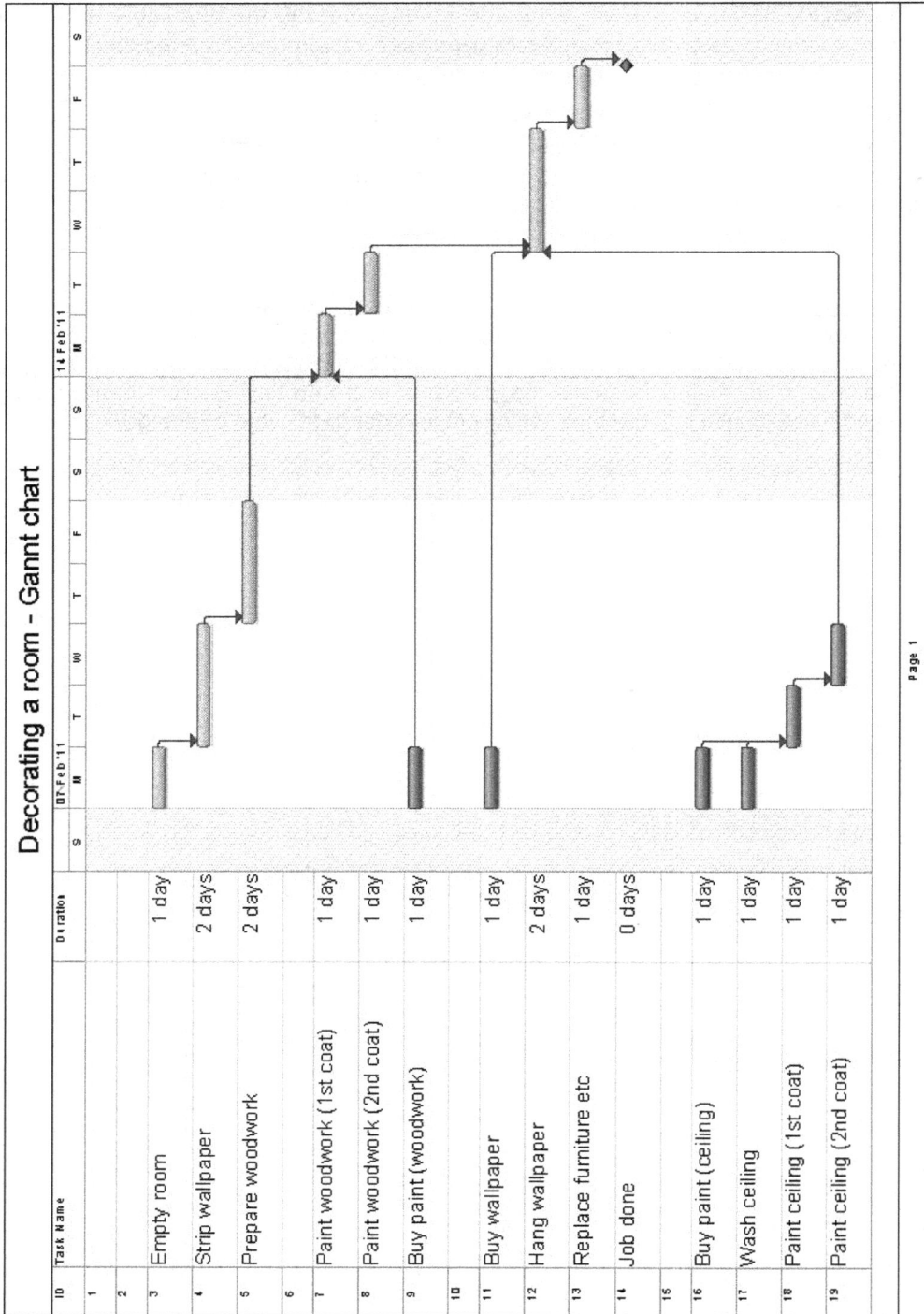

Decorating a room - Gannt chart

ID	Task Name	Duration
1		
2		
3	Empty room	1 day
4	Strip wallpaper	2 days
5	Prepare woodwork	2 days
6		
7	Paint woodwork (1st coat)	1 day
8	Paint woodwork (2nd coat)	1 day
9	Buy paint (woodwork)	1 day
10		
11	Buy wallpaper	1 day
12	Hang wallpaper	2 days
13	Replace furniture etc	1 day
14	Job done	0 days
15		
16	Buy paint (ceiling)	1 day
17	Wash ceiling	1 day
18	Paint ceiling (1st coat)	1 day
19	Paint ceiling (2nd coat)	1 day

PERT chart – decorating a room

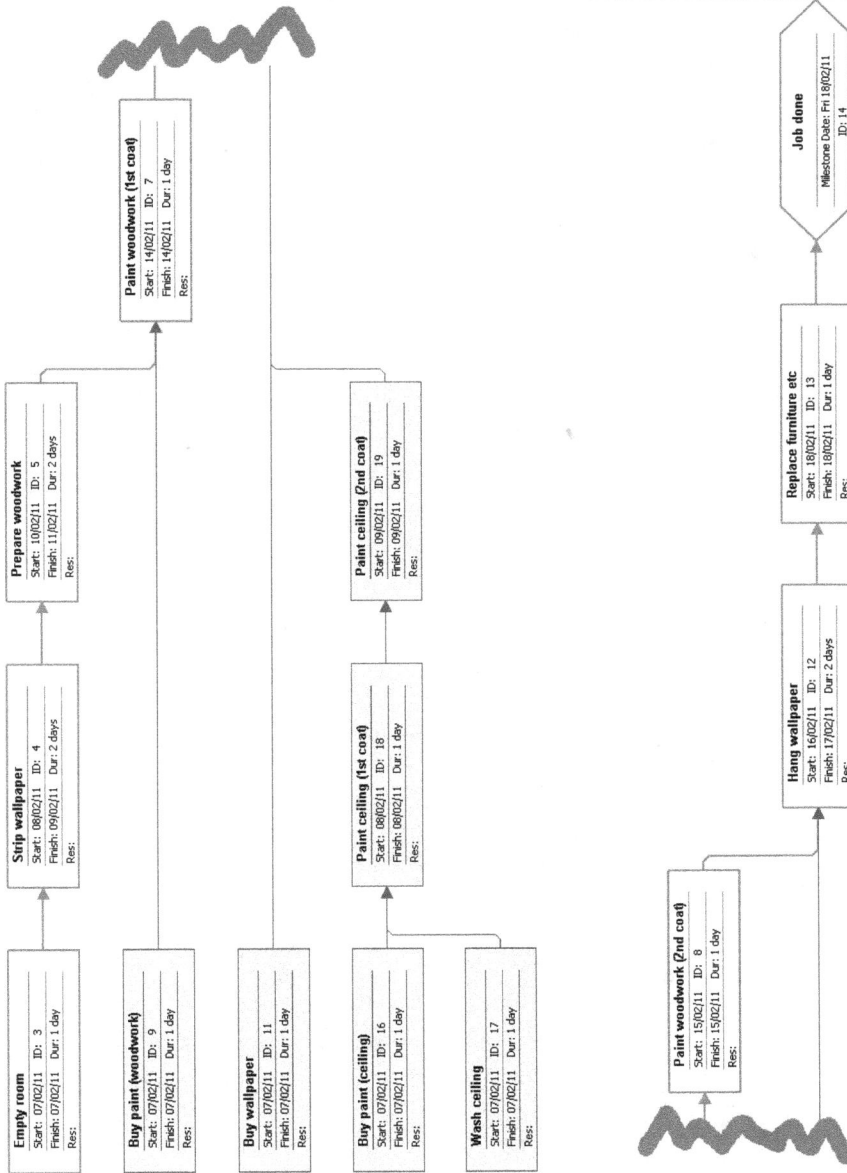

Empty room
Start: 07/02/11 ID: 3
Finish: 07/02/11 Dur: 1 day
Res:

Strip wallpaper
Start: 08/02/11 ID: 4
Finish: 09/02/11 Dur: 2 days
Res:

Prepare woodwork
Start: 10/02/11 ID: 5
Finish: 11/02/11 Dur: 2 days
Res:

Paint woodwork (1st coat)
Start: 14/02/11 ID: 7
Finish: 14/02/11 Dur: 1 day
Res:

Buy paint (woodwork)
Start: 07/02/11 ID: 9
Finish: 07/02/11 Dur: 1 day
Res:

Buy wallpaper
Start: 07/02/11 ID: 11
Finish: 07/02/11 Dur: 1 day
Res:

Paint ceiling (1st coat)
Start: 08/02/11 ID: 18
Finish: 08/02/11 Dur: 1 day
Res:

Paint ceiling (2nd coat)
Start: 09/02/11 ID: 19
Finish: 09/02/11 Dur: 1 day
Res:

Buy paint (ceiling)
Start: 07/02/11 ID: 16
Finish: 07/02/11 Dur: 1 day
Res:

Wash ceiling
Start: 07/02/11 ID: 17
Finish: 07/02/11 Dur: 1 day
Res:

Paint woodwork (2nd coat)
Start: 15/02/11 ID: 8
Finish: 15/02/11 Dur: 1 day
Res:

Hang wallpaper
Start: 16/02/11 ID: 12
Finish: 17/02/11 Dur: 2 days
Res:

Replace furniture etc
Start: 18/02/11 ID: 13
Finish: 18/02/11 Dur: 1 day
Res:

Job done
Milestone Date: Fri 18/02/11
ID: 14

135

Appendix 4 - Table of Discount Factors

Discount rate

Year	1%	2%	3%	4%	5%	6%	7%	8%	9%	10%	11%	12%	13%	14%	15%
0	1.000	1.000	1.000	1.000	1.000	1.000	1.000	1.000	1.000	1.000	1.000	1.000	1.000	1.000	1.000
1	0.990	0.980	0.971	0.962	0.952	0.943	0.935	0.926	0.917	0.909	0.901	0.893	0.885	0.877	0.870
2	0.980	0.961	0.943	0.925	0.907	0.890	0.873	0.857	0.842	0.826	0.812	0.797	0.783	0.769	0.756
3	0.971	0.942	0.915	0.889	0.864	0.840	0.816	0.794	0.772	0.751	0.731	0.712	0.693	0.675	0.658
4	0.961	0.924	0.888	0.855	0.823	0.792	0.763	0.735	0.708	0.683	0.659	0.636	0.613	0.592	0.572
5	0.951	0.906	0.863	0.822	0.784	0.747	0.713	0.681	0.650	0.621	0.593	0.567	0.543	0.519	0.497
6	0.942	0.888	0.837	0.790	0.746	0.705	0.666	0.630	0.596	0.564	0.535	0.507	0.480	0.456	0.432
7	0.933	0.871	0.813	0.760	0.711	0.665	0.623	0.583	0.547	0.513	0.482	0.452	0.425	0.400	0.376
8	0.923	0.853	0.789	0.731	0.677	0.627	0.582	0.540	0.502	0.467	0.434	0.404	0.376	0.351	0.327
9	0.914	0.837	0.766	0.703	0.645	0.592	0.544	0.500	0.460	0.424	0.391	0.361	0.333	0.308	0.284
10	0.905	0.820	0.744	0.676	0.614	0.558	0.508	0.463	0.422	0.386	0.352	0.322	0.295	0.270	0.247
11	0.896	0.804	0.722	0.650	0.585	0.527	0.475	0.429	0.388	0.350	0.317	0.287	0.261	0.237	0.215
12	0.887	0.788	0.701	0.625	0.557	0.497	0.444	0.397	0.356	0.319	0.286	0.257	0.231	0.208	0.187
13	0.879	0.773	0.681	0.601	0.530	0.469	0.415	0.368	0.326	0.290	0.258	0.229	0.204	0.182	0.163
14	0.870	0.758	0.661	0.577	0.505	0.442	0.388	0.340	0.299	0.263	0.232	0.205	0.181	0.160	0.141
15	0.861	0.743	0.642	0.555	0.481	0.417	0.362	0.315	0.275	0.239	0.209	0.183	0.160	0.140	0.123
16	0.853	0.728	0.623	0.534	0.458	0.394	0.339	0.292	0.252	0.218	0.188	0.163	0.141	0.123	0.107
17	0.844	0.714	0.605	0.513	0.436	0.371	0.317	0.270	0.231	0.198	0.170	0.146	0.125	0.108	0.093
18	0.836	0.700	0.587	0.494	0.416	0.350	0.296	0.250	0.212	0.180	0.153	0.130	0.111	0.095	0.081
19	0.828	0.686	0.570	0.475	0.396	0.331	0.277	0.232	0.194	0.164	0.138	0.116	0.098	0.083	0.070
20	0.820	0.673	0.554	0.456	0.377	0.312	0.258	0.215	0.178	0.149	0.124	0.104	0.087	0.073	0.061

Table 7 - Discount factors

Appendix 5 – Answer to critical path exercise

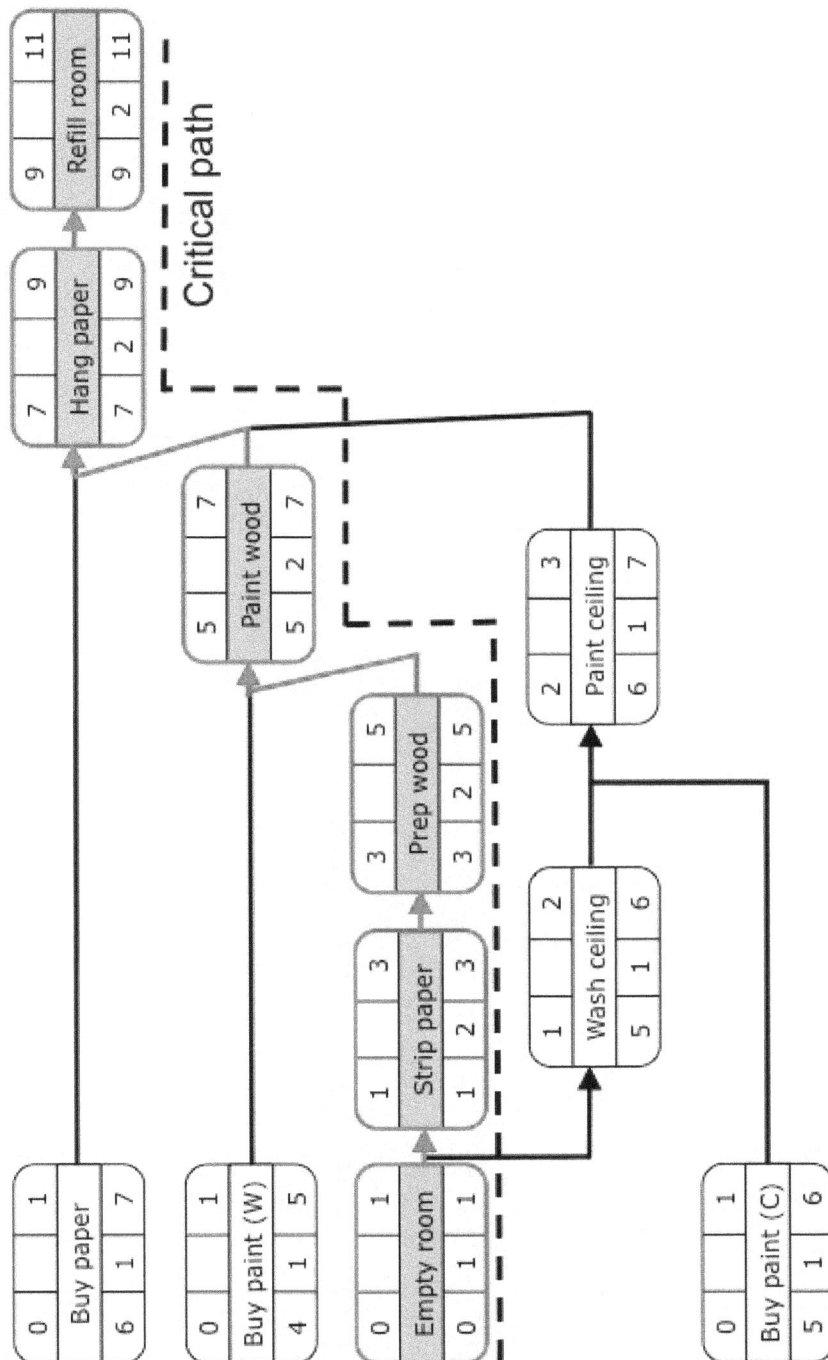

Index to tables

Table 1 – Project finance report 89
Table 2 - Simple cashflow calculation 123
Table 3 - Net cashflow for simple calculation 127
Table 4 - Present value calculation 128
Table 5 - Simple cashflow calculation: option 2 130
Table 6 - Comparison of NPVs... 130
Table 7 - Discount factors 136

Index to figures

Figure 1 – Dimensions of a project 6

Figure 2 – Six Stage Model 11

Figure 3 – Impact table 25

Figure 4 – Risk Register 26

Figure 5 – PERT chart 38

Figure 6 – Gannt chart 39

Figure 7 – Laying pipes: first draft 40

Figure 8 – Laying pipes: second draft 40

Figure 9 – Breakfast: network diagram 42

Figure 10 – Breakfast: Gannt chart 43

Figure 11 – Breakfast – add 'butter toast' 43

Figure 12 – Breakfast: network diagram 45

Figure 13 – Breakfast: critical path 45

Figure 14 – CPA: first stage 46

Figure 15 – Network diagram node 47

Figure 16 – CPA: time for tasks A & B added 47

Figure 17 – End and start times 47

Figure 18 – Back to back meetings 48

Figure 19 – CPA: third stage 48

Figure 20 – CPA: Forward pass completed 49

Figure 21 – CPA: starting reverse pass 49

Figure 22 – CPA: sixth stage 49

Figure 23 – CPA: reverse pass complete 50

Figure 24 – CPA: complete with critical path 50

Figure 25 – Levelling: stage one 55

Figure 26 – Levelling: stage two 56

Figure 27 – Levelling: stage three 57

Figure 28 – Levelling: stage four; 2 bathrooms 58

Figure 29 – Project Management in one diagram 71

Figure 30 – SOFT report 76

Figure 31 – Gannt chart as monitoring tool (1) 77

Figure 32 – Gannt chart as monitoring tool (2) 77

Figure 33 – Payback period 124

Figure 34 – NPV with discount rate 129

Figure 35 – Internal rate of return for Option 1 131

INDEX

80/20 rule, 44, 111

Acceptance, 17, 27, 33, 95, 97
  certificate, 96
  criteria, 30, 84, 95, 97, 109
Achievable/Agreed, 13
Adair, John, 87
Articulation, 13, 29
Association of Project Managers, 115
Audio conference, 81

Back up, 103
  restore, 104
Beef stew, 35
Belbin, 68, 70
Blog, 2, 82, 85, 86, 87
Brainstorm, 18, 24, 46, 92
Brevity, 87
Budget, 4, 5, 10, 21, 22, 23, 28, 54, 60,
  61, 62, 63, 64, 66, 67, 73, 75, 83, 88,
  90, 96, 97, 105, 110, 113, 114
  presenting, 89
  variances, 74
Bulletin board, 85
Business Case
  initial, 29

Cashflow, 20, 90, 123, 125, 128
Change, 3, 4, 13, 18, 24, 26, 27, 28, 30,
  32, 33, 36, 41, 45, 53, 64, 83, 88, 93,
  97, 98, 101, 107, 125
  control, 83, 105, 109
  control mantra, 84
  post project update, 84
  project drift, 97
  request, 105
  request log, 84, 109
Chart
  Gannt, 37, 38, 40, 43, 76, 115, 134
  PERT, 37, 38, 41, 76, 135
Clarity, 79, 84, 87
Close/handover, 9
Closure, 96, 97, 99
  meeting, 97
Cloud computing, 86
Communication, 3, 9, 66, 68, 81, 85, 86,
  106, 109, 110
  effective, 87
  plan, 29, 87
  type, 85
Completer Finisher (Belbin), 70

Conclusion, 96
  successful, 95
Conference
  audio, 78, 81
  room, 52
  video, 78, 82
Contingency, 5, 26, 27, 63, 64
  budgeting, 60
  plan, 23, 25, 106
Control, 9, 27, 30, 71, 83
  change, 83, 105, 109
  change control mantra, 84
  mechanisms, 106
  process, 83
  project, 29
Co-ordinator (Belbin), 70
Cost, 12, 20, 27, 36, 54, 81, 88
  benefit, 21, 29
  budgeting, 60, 61, 64
  centres, 96
  change, 93
  contingency, 63
  data loss, 103
  development, 22
  full cost recovery, 60
  human resource, 62
  in DCF example, 123
  meeting, 63, 80, 82
  of risk, 27
  on-costs, 60
  operational, 22
  project drift, 97
  project manager, 63
  quality, 61
  software, 100
  travel, 63
Cost/benefit, 21
Critical Path, 43, 44, 45, 50, 59, 88, 121
  analysis, 44, 46
  definition, 44
  software, 64
  worked example, 46
Crystal ball, 15, 113
Customer, 4, 5, 8, 17, 18, 29, 33, 67, 69,
  72, 83, 84, 85, 92, 93, 94, 95, 97, 98,
  101, 108, 109

Define, 9, 10, 13, 17, 32, 34, 92
Deliverable, 12, 29, 30, 33, 62, 68, 113
Dependencies, 36, 37, 38, 39, 41, 44, 51,
  52, 58, 59, 102, 121
Discount, 7, 101
  factor, 126, 127, 136

141

rate, 125, 126, 127, 128, 129, 131
Discounted cash flow, 22, 123, 127
Duration, 35, 38, 39, 41, 45, 46, 47, 60, 95, 121
  estimating, 61

Early finish, 46
Early start, 46
Effort, 35, 92
Eisenhower
  Dwight. D, 32
Emergence, 12, 29
Empathy, 87
Estimating, 61, 63
Evaluate, 9
Evaluation, 38, 98
  meeting, 90
  review, 97
Exit, 9
  handover, 95
  strategy, 30

Facebook, 85
Facilitation, 67
Failure, 66, 75, 76, 113
Feasibility, 12, 20
  environmental, 20
  financial, 20
  managerial, 20
  social, 20
  technical, 20
  value related, 20
File and forget, 98
Float, 42, 45
Forward pass, 48
Funding, 3, 7, 13, 15, 20, 30, 60, 96, 98

Garbage in, Garbage out (GIGO), 65, 100
Goal Displacement, 33
Golden rules, 6, 87

Handing over, 109
  the keys, 4, 95
Handover, 95, 96

Impact
  analysis, 24
  table, 25
Implement, 9
Implementer (Belbin), 70
Influencing, 66
Interest rates, 125, 131
Internal rate of return, 129, 131

iPod, 86
Issue, 6, 8, 27, 29, 57, 68, 72, 73, 75, 78, 80, 83, 84, 91, 92, 93, 95, 107, 108, 109, 111
  log, 8, 107, 109
  outstanding, 97
  register, 8, 18, 105
  report, 91, 105, 107, 108, 109
  unresolved, 95

Key steps, 32, 34
KISS, 6, 87

Late finish, 46
Late start, 46
Leadership, 66, 68
Levelling, 52, 54
  realistic, 53
  resource limited, 53
  time limited, 53
Liability, 24
Linking tasks, 39
  Finish-Finish, 39
  Finish-Start, 39
  Start-Start, 39
Log book, 8, 71, 74

MBWA, 73, 88
Measurable, 13
Meetings, 7, 8, 26, 48, 61, 79, 80, 81, 85, 98, 106, 110
  cost of, 80
  net, 78, 82
  project, 78
  review, 29
  risk review, 106
  successful, 78
  virtual, 78
Methodology, 7
Michelangelo, 16
Microsoft Project, 51, 55, 64, 76, 100, 102
Milestone, 30, 55, 72, 95
  gate, 72
Models, 9
Monitor Evaluator (Belbin), 70
Monitoring, 3, 71, 72, 74, 77
Motivation, 67
mp3, 86
Multiple projects, 111, 112
Multi-site projects, 109

Negotiation, 28, 67
Net present value, 128

Network diagram, 37, 42, 50
Newsletter, 60, 76, 85
No surprises, 6, 51, 74, 106

Objectives, 3, 10, 12, 13, 14, 15, 16, 17,
    19, 21, 23, 28, 30, 31, 67, 79, 90, 98,
    113, 118
    realistic, 14
    SMART, 13, 29, 67
Opportunities, 20, 70, 75, 76, 106
Outcome, 14, 15, 17, 33, 97
Output, 14, 19, 36, 54, 97
Outstanding
    issue, 95, 97

Paperwork, 74, 105, 107
Pareto Principle, 44
Payback period, 123, 130
Plan, 9
Planning, 1, 10, 12, 20, 23, 29, 32, 54,
    59, 68, 95, 107, 111
    at the computer, 102
    budget, 60
    contingency, 64, 106
Plant (Belbin), 70
Podcast, 85, 86
Politics, 66
Portfolio of success, 96, 98
Post-It, 41, 46
Predecessor, 39, 44
Present value, 125, 128
PRINCE2, 7, 8, 9, 32, 75
Priorities, 26, 59, 66, 111
Problems, 8, 68, 70, 78, 81, 84, 88, 90,
    91, 92, 93, 97, 107, 108
    communication, 106
Product, 5, 21, 29, 32, 33, 34, 35, 67, 84,
    97
Progress, 67, 71, 72, 75, 76, 77, 78, 80,
    88, 111
Project, 1
    background, 29
    board, 17
    brief, 1, 3, 8, 12, 29, 94, 105
    budget, 22
    budget planning, 60
    change, 83, 93
    closure, 96
    communication, 66, 85
    control, 71, 83
    define, 12
    definition, 3, 29
    dimensions, 4, 6

    drift, 97
    evaluation, 90, 98
    finances, 90
    gestation, 12
    handover, 95
    initiation document, 12, 29
    issue, 91
    kick-off, 30
    large, 105
    levelling, 54
    life cycle, 9
    manager, 1, 2, 5, 7, 17, 18, 66, 105
    meetings, 78
    methodology, 7
    milestone, 72
    objective, 33
    objectives, 12, 13, 14, 67
    organisation, 29
    people, 17
    plan, 8, 105
    planning, 107
    Polaris, 38
    quality, 61
        plan, 29
    records, 8
    reports, 101
    resource, 52
        costs, 62
    review, 80, 85, 88
    risks, 23, 27, 88
    scheduling, 36
    scope, 5
    sign-off, 95
    SOFT report, 75
    software, 7, 64, 100
    specification, 8, 12, 29
    sponsor, 12
    stakeholder, 4, 17
    team, 17, 18, 21, 66, 68, 106
    time slippage, 73
    tracking, 75, 76
    what can go wrong, 113
    write-up, 98
Project finance report, 89
Project Management Institute, 115
Projects
    multiple, 111

Quality, 5, 21, 29, 53, 60
Question, 13, 71, 72, 73, 75, 88, 89, 92,
    98

Realistic, 13

Recognition, 13
Relationship management, 66
Resource, 12, 17, 21, 27, 30, 34, 35, 36, 40, 41, 52, 53, 54, 55, 60, 62, 64, 67, 77, 88, 97, 101, 105, 111, 113, 133
Resource Investigator (Belbin), 70
Restore data, 104
Reverse pass, 49
Review, 9, 10, 15, 18, 26, 38, 80, 81, 85, 88
  budget, 88
  evaluation, 97
  meetings, 29, 106
  need, 90
  plan, 88
  project, 80
  risk, 88
  stage, 107
Risk, 4, 6, 23, 75, 78, 80, 119, 131
  acceptance, 27
  analysis, 24
  change, 27
  contingency, 27
  cost, 27
  fiscal, 24
  labour, 24
  liability, 24
  log, 8, 30, 88, 105
  physical, 23
  planning, 106
  political, 24
  prevention, 26
  reduction, 27
  register, 1, 8, 18, 26, 105, 109, 120
  review, 106
  socal, 24
  strategies, 26
  technical, 23
  transference, 27
Roles, 29, 68, 70

Salami technique, 36
Schedule, 5, 26, 30, 34, 36, 37, 41, 43, 52, 53, 56, 58, 66, 74, 75, 76, 80, 88, 113
  acid test, 36
  checklist, 58
Scheduling, 36, 64
Scope, 4, 5, 29, 53, 54, 67, 80, 83, 84, 90, 93, 110, 113
Self development, 99
Senior management, 24, 54, 60, 69, 72, 105, 123, 128

Shaper (Belbin), 70
Sharepoint, 85
Six stage model, 11
Slippage, 72, 73
SMART, 13, 14, 15, 29, 67, 118
Social media, 85, 86
SOFT report, 75, 76
Software, 7, 36, 41, 43, 50, 53, 55, 61, 64, 65, 85, 96, 100, 101, 102, 103, 107, 111
Specialist (Belbin), 70
Specific, 13
Sponsor, 12, 17, 83, 84, 96, 97, 99
Stakeholder, 4, 13, 17, 18, 21, 29, 30, 75, 76, 83, 85, 86, 87, 93, 94, 97
  log/register, 8
  register, 18
Status report, 75
Structured approach, 7, 100
Stuart's mean beef stew, 35
Success, 66, 68, 75, 76, 96, 98, 113, 114
Suppliers, 17, 98, 100, 103
Surprises, 6, 7, 51, 74, 75, 78, 99, 106

Team, 67
Team building, 9
Teamworker (Belbin), 70
Terms of reference, 29
Threats, 20, 75, 76, 106
Time, 54, 78, 79, 80, 81, 83, 87, 88, 91, 93, 98, 101, 105, 110, 113, 123
Timely, 13
To heck with it!, 31
Tracking progress, 71, 75, 76
Trustees, 6, 12, 17, 21, 54, 69, 75, 105, 123, 128
Twitter, 85, 86, 87

Video conference, 81, 82
Volunteers, 63

Web, 1, 5, 12, 29, 82, 85, 86
What can go wrong, 113
Wiki, 85

www.ingramcontent.com/pod-product-compliance
Lightning Source LLC
Chambersburg PA
CBHW080615270326
41928CB00016B/3071